Discourse Analysis:
Recurrent Intonation Patterns
in the Kennedy / Nixon Debates

ScriptOralia **4**

Herausgegeben von
Paul Goetsch, Wolfgang Raible und Hans-Robert Roemer

Katherina Nanov-Schwehr

Discourse Analysis: Recurrent Intonation Patterns in the Kennedy/Nixon Debates

gnV Gunter Narr Verlag Tübingen

CIP-Titelaufnahme der Deutschen Bibliothek

Nanov-Schwehr, Katharina:
Discourse analysis: recurrent intonation patterns in the Kennedy, Nixon debates / Katharina Nanov-Schwehr. – Tübingen : Narr, 1988.
(Script-Oralia ; 4)
ISBN 3-87808-394-7 kart.
ISBN 3-87808-797-7 geb.

NE: GT

Druck und Verarbeitung: Weihert-Druck GmbH, Darmstadt
Printed in Germany

ISBN 3-87808-797-7 (geb.)
ISBN 3-87808-394-7 (kt.)

To my parents and Helmut for their moral support.

My special thanks go to Professor Herbert Pilch for encouraging me in this endeavor and his continued support and critical interest in its progress.

I would also like to thank my students at the University of Freiburg and my colleagues, in particular Dr. Elizabeth Couper-Kuhlen, Dr. Janet Harkness, Dr. Axel Koberne, Dr. Richard Matthews and David Mace, for allowing themselves to be inveigled into discussions on intonation and for their valuable suggestions on interpreting my empirical data.

Last but not least my thanks go to Helmut Schwehr not only for his help and advice but also for the gentle nudges in the right direction.

TABLE OF CONTENTS

Herbert Pilch

Preface

Intonation is **the** hallmark of orality vs. literacy. All other language structures are present both in the phonic and the graphic substance. Intonation is present only in the phonic, but not in the graphic substance. All this is generally accepted at least as far as alphabetic writing is concerned as commonly practised in Europe. What we might argue about are minor matters. Doesn't punctuation signal intonation? Let alone graphic devices such as italics, spacing, capitalization, parentheses? Sure, but in a very rudimentary fashion. Isn't "the presence" of language structures "in the phonic substance" a misnomer, theoretically speaking? Maybe, but let's agree (everyone's pet theory notwithstanding) that *present* in the above phrase just means 'available to linguistic analysis'.

A major objection hinges on the fact that certain texts have obviously been conceived as oral (even though they have been "reduced to writing", the present preface is one of them) and, inversely, some other texts have obviously been conceived as written (even though they are being read aloud, many learned papers read at congresses are of this kind). So, is the substance (phonic vs. graphic), perhaps, just accidental? The essence of orality vs. literacy being somewhere else? For instance in the amount of "distance" between speakers? Distance not only in the literal sense, but also in the metaphorical sense of intimacy (oral) vs. detachment (written)?[1] Non Sequitur.

On the contrary - if the oral quality were, in fact, an abstract quantity such as "amount of distance" (regardless of substance), how come those written congress papers are so hard to understand when read aloud? How come "reducing" orality to writing (e.g. transcribing a debate for the printing press) is such a big problem? We'd suggest that the written paper has a soporific effect when it IS read aloud, precisely because it has been conceived without intonation. Inversely, the oral paper is such a problem to the press editor, because the intonation cannot be rendered in writing. Consequently, the transcript easily misses focus, even lacks coherence. So far, the oral (vs. written) quality is obviously linked to the substance. If, instead, it were linked to some quantifiable abstraction, why should the transfer to the opposite substance make such a difference?

[1] Cf. Peter Koch, Wulf Oesterreicher, "Sprache der Nähe - Sprache der Distanz. Mündlichkeit und Schriftlichkeit im Spannungsfeld von Sprachtheorie und Sprachgeschichte," *Romanistisches Jahrbuch,* 36 (1985), 1-38.

Less obviously, speech communities observe different linguistic conventions in oral and written speech even in morphology, syntax and the lexicon. A morphological case in point is the proclitic *g'na*-future of English (as in *I'm g'na argue*, this future is generally current in oral English, it is neither specifically American vs. British nor specific to any particular social stratum). Two syntagms in point are the reduplicative syntagm[2] and the tag syntagm[3]. The German diminutives in *-chen* (such as *Frauchen, Mannchen, Hundchen*) are a lexical example. They are productive (without *umlaut* of the stem) in spoken Northern German.[4]

Speakers (and writers) who put those different conventions to advantage are applauded as good speakers (and writers respectively). Those who do not are mediocre speakers, those who mix the conventions are poor speakers (witness the unskilled reader of a written paper). In fact, in order to appropriately read aloud a written paper, one has to do a lot of editing - quite as much editing as in the inverse case. Both the good speaker and the poor speaker observe the same grammar rules, of course. So the difference is not in grammar rules. It is in the choice of the appropriate conventions, and therefore a matter not of rule, but of free choice[5].

What are, then, those conventions that the good speaker chooses in order to put across his message? The answer cannot be in the choice of specific syntagms or specific pitch patterns, because these can be used to put across (or not put across) **any** message. We believe the answer is in the way those linguistic structures are used to establish textual coherence. Kenneth L. Pike has modeled textual coherence in terms of "generalized plots" signaled by specific "plot cues"[6]. The plot cues are specific linguistic structures, notably particles (such as *too, indeed, for example*) and pitch configurations. The

[2] Herbert Pilch, "Pour une syntaxe de la langue parlée: La construction anglaise à redoublement," *Festschrift O. Szemerényi,* ed. B. Brogyanyi (Amsterdam, 1979), 655-661.

[3] Herbert Pilch, "The tag syntagm of spoken English," *Festschrift J. Fisiak, Linguistic across Historical and Geographical Boundaries, 2: Descriptive, Contrastive and Applied Linguistics,* ed. D. Kastovsky and A. Szwedek (Berlin, 1986), 983-991.

[4] Herbert Pilch, "Dialectology in Historical Grammar," Proceedings of the Conference on Historical Dialectology held at Blażewejko May 8-10, 1986, ed. J. Fisiak, Berlin (to appear).

[5] Herbert Pilch, "Von der Freiheit eines Sprechers," *Festschrift Peter Hartmann* (Tübingen, 1982), 17-22.

[6] Cf. K. Nanov-Schwehr, ch. 1.2.2. below.

generalized plots, on the other hand, are not language-specific, but can be signaled in any language that has the appropriate cues, e. g. the plot *general statement : examples.*

John F. Kennedy and Richard M. Nixon doubtless were/are good speakers. In their election debate of 1960, either put across his message. Katherina Nanov-Schwehr has found empirical motivation in this debate to set up an open set of generalized plots, as signaled by intonational cues. She abandons the search for "grammar rules" such as the traditional rise for yes-or-no questions, fall for statements and *wh*-questions. What she sets up are, necessarily, *models* of generalized plots, not hypotheses of the format: "plot p_1 is signaled by cue *x*". The search for hypotheses of the latter type is pointless, precisely because the speakers exercise free choice. Even good speakers are not rulebound, but free to choose their cues, and bad speakers will likely fail to observe the appropriate conventions, for instance monotonously read aloud a written text.

Katherina Nanov-Schwehr's thesis is a pioneering effort. So there is justification for her limiting herself to a closed corpus. Her results are (as my own observations suggest) borne out well beyond the limited corpus. The closed corpus does provide empirical motivation only for a small subset of models. Again, this is justifiable in a pioneering effort which provides not only models of intonational plots, but a model to be followed by more researchers to complete the open subset.

Being as it is the hallmark of orality vs. literacy, intonation is, appropriately, the dominant theme of orality research. All those other problems that result from the transfer to the opposite substance invariably involve intonation. Paul Goetsch's "fictitious orality" in the written novel involves the novelist's attempt to suggest what his character's speech sounds like[7]. The noted dichotomy, in versification, of metre vs. rhythm involves the manifestation of a metrical pattern in terms of intonation. The oral literature of the Middle Ages is one which was at one time transmitted with intonation, but is extant without it today (to the extent that it IS extant). Learning to write involves learning the conventions of the graphic substance. However, very little is known so far about the communicative function of intonation apart from time-honored platitudes (such as the rules of question intonation) which are easily refuted by empirical observation. Katherina Nanov-Schwehr is breaking new ground.

[7]Cf. Paul Goetsch, "Fingierte Mündlichkeit in der Erzählkunst entwickelter Schriftkulturen," *Poetica*, 17 (1985), 202-218.

1. INTRODUCTION

1.1 Statement of the Problem

In this thesis we are investigating if *discourse structure* is signalled by intonational cues and, if so, what these intonational cues are. Our method of approaching this problem is empirical: We a) make observations, b) formulate working hypotheses, and c) test these working hypotheses against additional data, i. e. we rely on further observations to validate or falsify our working hypotheses. We observe, for example, that Richard M. Nixon uses a *rising pitch* in his opening statement to cue the *yes-no* question *Does this mean that his program is better than ours?* and hypothesize that *rising pitch* co-occurs with *yes-no* questions, i. e. that there is a CO-OCCURRENCE RELATION between *rising pitch* and *yes-no* questions. To validate or falsify this working hypothesis we must take into account all *yes-no* questions included in our data.

Our empirical data is taken from John F. Kennedy's and Richard M. Nixon's opening statements in the 1960 presidential debates. This data is presented in the appendix. A brief summary and analysis of each candidate's opening statement, pointing out respective rhetorical and intonational characteristics, helps to elucidate the empirical data. An exhaustive account is not intended.

A preliminary to any such analysis is the necessity of defining one's terms:

1) What principles are essential to the organization of an effective discourse?; And, what constitutes discourse structure?

2) What intonational means does the speaker have at his disposal for signalling discourse structure, i. e. to help transmit his message? The answer to this question entails a short description of the intonation model being used for the analysis.

1.2 Discourse Structure

1.2.1 Principles of Organization: Unity, Coherence, Emphasis

What principles are essential to the organization of an effective discourse?[1] According to Brooks and Warren there are three such principles of organization: UNITY, COHERENCE, and EMPHASIS.[2] The terms *unity* and *coherence* are related. A distinction, however, can be made between them. The key to this distinction is the word *order*. "In unity, the emphasis is on the relation of the various elements of a discourse to the dominant topic"[3], i. e. the minor topics should be kept subordinated to the main topic, which, in turn, should permeate the whole discourse. "In coherence, the emphasis is on the order - the continuity - of the elements."[4] The elements of a discourse, in other words, must be logically integrated, they must hang together if they are to form a unified whole (i. e. a TEXT)[5], rather than merely a disconnected string of sentences. This automatically raises the following question: What means exist in English for making a text hang together, i. e. for achieving coherence?

One way of establishing coherence is through the repetition of lexical items.[6] Halliday and Hasan speak of LEXICAL REITERATION in this connection and state that "lexical reiteration takes place not only through repetition of

---

[1] In accord with Brooks and Warren we define discourse as a formal communication. Cf. Cleanth Brooks and Robert Penn Warren, *Modern Rhetoric* (New York, 1979), p. 21, n. 1.

[2] *Ibid.*, p. 21.

[3] *Ibid.*, p. 25.

[4] *Ibid.*, p. 25.

[5] We are adopting Halliday and Hasan's definition of *text*, which reads as follows: "The word TEXT is used in linguistics to refer to any passage, spoken or written, of whatever length, that does form a unified whole." Cf. M. A. K. Halliday and Ruqaiya Hasan, *Cohesion in English* (London, 1976), p. 1.

[6] For an exhaustive account cf. Halliday and Hasan. They set up the concept of COHESION to account for relations in discourse and define this concept as follows: "Cohesion refers to the range of possibilities that exist for linking something with what has gone before." Cf. Halliday and Hasan, *op. cit.*, p. 10. According to Halliday and Hasan there are five types of cohesion: REFERENCE, SUBSTITUTION, ELLIPSIS, CONJUNCTION and LEXICAL COHESION.

an identical lexical item but also through occurrence of a different lexical item that is systematically related to the first one, as a synonym [*obligations ... responsibilities*] or a superordinate of it [*nation ... world*]."[7] To account for the relationship between pairs of words such as *stand still ... move ahead* (complementaries) and *individually ... collectively* (antonyms), Halliday and Hasan extend the basis of the lexical relationship that features as a cohesive force and say that "there is cohesion between any pair of lexical items that stand to each other in some recognizable lexico-semantic (word meaning) relation."[8] They refer to this type of lexical cohesion as COLLOCATION.[9]

To avoid repetition of lexical items the speaker can resort to the following two syntactic devices for connecting sentences:

1) ELLIPSIS.[10] An example of *ellipsis* are lines 105-107 of Kennedy's opening statement.[11] The lexical items *developed the Tennessee Valley* are ellipted (i. e. omitted) in the antithesis *collectively they could have*:

   The people of the United States, individually, could not have developed the Tennessee Valley, collectively they could have (*developed the Tennessee Valley*).

2) SUBSTITUTION by PRO-FORMS, such as pronouns or *do* etc.[12] In line 112 of his opening statement Kennedy substitutes the pro-form *do so* to avoid

[7] *Ibid.*, p. 284.

[8] *Ibid.*, p. 285.

[9] *Ibid.*, pp. 284-288. For a detailed account on lexical cohesion compare Halliday and Hasan, chapter 6. Cf. also in this connection Randolph Quirk, Sidney Greenbaum, Geoffrey Leech and Jan Svartvik, *A Grammar of Contemporary English* (London, 1972), pp. 653-655, who speak of LEXICAL EQUIVALENCE, and Richard E. Young, Alton L. Becker, and Kenneth L. Pike, *Rhetoric: Discovery and Change* (New York, 1970), pp. 346-348, who speak of LEXICAL CHAIN LINKING. We adopt Young, Becker and Pike's technical term LEXICAL CHAIN (cf. ch. 1.2.2.), but re-define it to include those lexical items which Halliday and Hasan group under the heading of *collocational cohesion*.

[10] Cf. Quirk *et al.*, *op. cit.*, pp. 583 ff. and pp. 707-715.

[11] This type of ellipsis is known as *zeugma* in classical rhetoric. Cf. Heinrich F. Plett, *Einführung in die rhetorische Textanalyse* (Hamburg, 1973), p. 57, and Heinrich Lausberg, *Handbuch der literarischen Rhetorik* (München, 1960), pp. 346-353, § 688-708.

[12] Cf. Quirk *et al.*, *op. cit.*, pp. 677-700.

repetition of *protect himself against the forces of supply and demand in the market place*:

> A cotton farmer in Georgia or a peanut farmer or a dairy farmer in Wisconsin or Minnesota, he cannot protect himself against the forces of supply and demand in the market place, but working together in effective governmental programs he can *do so*.

Other syntactic means for achieving coherence are:

a) the use of items having the property of 'deictic' reference, i. e. the use of items which point back (ANAPHORIC) or forward (CATAPHORIC) in discourse.[13] An example of *anaphoric* reference is:

> *These* are all the things I think in this country that can make our society strong or can mean that it stands still.

These refers anaphorically (i. e. points back) to all the examples Kennedy has given of where he's dissatisfied with America's progress (ll. 49–82).

An example of *cataphoric* reference is:

> I think it will depend in great measure upon what we do *here* in the United States.

Here refers cataphorically (i. e. points forward) to the United States.

b) the use of connectives that indicate the structure of thought, such as: *for example* – introduces an illustration; *but* – introduces a contradiction; *of course* – makes a concession, etc. These are Halliday and Hasan's CONJUNCTIVE ELEMENTS, Quirk's LOGICAL CONNECTERS.[14] Young, Becker and Pike refer to PLOT CUES in this connection (cf. ch. 1.2.2.).

c) the use of adverbials or adjectives that signal time-relationships. We cite the following example from Kennedy's opening statement:

> The Chinese communists have always had a large population, but they are important and dangerous *now* ...

---

[13] *Ibid.*, pp. 700-706.

[14] Cf. Halliday and Hasan, *op. cit.*, ch. 5, and Quirk *et al.*, *op. cit.*, pp. 661-677.

Now signals "temporal ordering simultaneous with given time-reference."[15] The given time-reference is the time at which Kennedy is making his opening statement, i. e. the year 1960.

d) by syntactic parallelism as in the following example:[16]

> ... on the kind of society that we build,
> on the kind of strength that we maintain.

Let us sum up. Above, we have briefly digressed from our topic to point out some of the devices available to the speaker for making his discourse coherent. The use of such devices and adherence to the principle of unity are essential to the organization of an effective discourse. Also essential to the organization of an effective discourse, but in a different sense, is the third member of the triad - *emphasis* (see ch. 1.2.1.). *Emphasis* can be defined as special prominence given to certain elements in a discourse so as to make them stand out. The 'proper' use of emphasis[17] is a "very important aspect of the mastery of forceful discourse."[18] Its intelligent control makes for good rhetoric, preventing a discourse from becoming monotonous.

The means of expressing emphasis are numerous. Repetition of an idea, for example, can give it prominence. The repetition must be combined with some progression in the treatment of the subject, however, if it is to be effective. We are primarily concerned with intonational means of expressing emphasis (cf. the appendix) and such stylistic means as ANADIPLOSIS and FOREGROUNDING.

Anadiplosis is "the repetition of a key word, especially the last one, at the beginning of the next sentence or clause"[19], as in line 9 of Nixon's opening statement:

> ... because we are in a deadly competition, a *competition* not
> only with the men in the Kremlin ...

The term *foregrounding* was coined by Jan Mukařovský, a chief proponent of the concept of style as deviance - the idea that style is constituted

---

[15]Quirk *et. al., op. cit.*, p. 657, ch. 10.12.

[16]Cf. *ibid.*, pp. 715-716.

[17]Note that we stress the 'proper' use of emphasis. Too much emphasis ends up by being 'no' emphasis at all.

[18]Brooks and Warren, *op. cit.*, p. 228.

[19]*Webster's New World Dictionary of the American Language*, College Edition, (New York, 1962), p. 52.

by violations of linguistic norms.[20] Mukařovský defines *foregrounding* as "the deautomatization of an act,"[21] or the deautomatization of language, in other words. "Everyday usage, according to Mukařovský, 'automatizes' or conventionalizes language to the point that its users no longer perceive its expressive or aesthetic potential; ..."[22] Language is used not for its own sake, but solely for the purpose of communication. It is the function of *poetic language* to 'deautomatize' or 'foreground' language, i. e. to push communication into the background and "place in the foreground the act of expression, the act of speech itself."[23] It can do so only by violating the norms of everyday language, according to Mukařovský: "The violation of the norm of the standard, its systematic violation, is what makes possible the poetic utilization of language; without this possibility there would be no poetry."[24]

Foregrounding is not only a trait of *poetic language*, it is also common in the *standard language*, as in Kennedy's and Nixon's opening statements, for example. Here, however, it is subordinate to communication, its purpose being "to attract the reader's (listener's) attention more closely to the subject matter expressed by the foregrounded means of expression."[25] An example of foregrounding in our text is line 105 of Kennedy's opening statement. To focus his audience's attention on the topic individual vs. governmental action Kennedy foregrounds the lexical item *individually*, i. e. he moves this lexical item from its normal syntactic position at the end of the sentence to a more prominent position:[26]

> The people of the United States, *individually*, could not have developed the Tennessee Valley ...

---

[20]Cf. Elizabeth C. Traugott and Mary L. Pratt, *Linguistics for Students of Literature* (New York, 1980), p. 31.

[21]Jan Mukařovský, "Standard Language and Poetic Language", in *A Prague School Reader on Esthetics, Literary Structure and Style*, trans. and ed. Paul Garvin (Washington, D. C., 1964), p. 19.

[22]Traugott and Pratt, *op. cit.*, p. 31.

[23]Mukařovský, *op. cit.*, p. 19.

[24]*Ibid.*, p. 18.

[25]*Ibid.*, p. 19.

[26]The foregrounding of *individually* is also effected by intonational means. Cf. our analysis in ch. 2., ex. 34.

1.2.2 Coherence and Discourse Structure

Certain items which are functional in establishing coherence are also necessary components in what we believe constitutes DISCOURSE STRUCTURE.[27] We may now ask: How many and of what type are the components which constitute discourse structure? Defining what we mean by discourse structure should help us to answer this question. The term *discourse structure* as such implies that there is an overall pattern in discourse. One way of discovering the overall pattern in any piece of discourse is by summarizing what it, in effect, is about.

According to Young, Becker and Pike "the act of summarizing is much like stating the plot of a play."[28] To illustrate what they mean by this assertion they present a summary of the story of Shakespeare's *Hamlet* and call this summary, with its particular cast, setting and actions, the *specific plot* of *Hamlet*. They then present a brief summary of a story about a boy in Alaska, which has an overall pattern identical to that in *Hamlet* – upon discovering that a wolf has killed his dog, the boy in Alaska, like Hamlet when he discovers that his uncle and mother have killed his father, wants to take revenge, formulates a plan, takes revenge and dies. Young, Becker and Pike give these two brief summaries to indicate that the stories share semantic patterns and call the semantic pattern that they share the *generalized plot*, which they define as follows: "A generalized plot is made up of a sequence of semantic slots which may be filled with a variety of specific semantic elements provided that the choice of an element to fill one slot is appropriate to the choices made for the other slots."[29] They continue by stating that other modes of writing (i. e. other kinds of discourse) also have generalized plots, but speak of 'recurring' generalized plots in this connection or "patterns that organize sentences into a whole unit."[30] These 'recurring' generalized plots are precisely what constitute discourse structure: they provide the framework that structures the specific elements of a discourse.

---

[27] In this connection we are primarily concerned with coherence by connectives and by reiteration (as discussed in ch. 1.2.1.).

[28] Young, Becker and Pike, *op. cit.*, p. 319.

[29] *Ibid.*, p. 319.

[30] *Ibid.*, p. 320.

Young, Becker and Pike give an illustrative list of such recurring generalized plots and the *plot cues* related to each[31], i. e. the specific set of words and phrases whose function it is "to mark the relationships of units within plots."[32] These plot cues are none other than our connectives for establishing coherence (cf. ch. 1.2.1.). Their function in discourse is to cue recurring patterns, or, in Young, Becker and Pike's terminology, the *generalized plots*.

For our analysis of discourse structure we adopt Young, Becker and Pike's term plot cues, but refer to them as OVERT PLOT CUES. We introduce the term *overt* to indicate that these plot cues are the conventional devices a speaker has at his disposal for marking relationships of units within plots. The speaker, however, is not constrained to use these conventional cues to convey these relationships. The generalized plot *B is a restatement of A* (i. e. STATEMENT : RESTATEMENT) is topically signalled by the plot cue *that is* or *in other words*, etc. Neither Kennedy nor Nixon use these or analogous plot cues to signal their restatements. Nixon uses primarily intonational cues to signal his restatements (cf. our analysis of Nixon's opening statement and the appendix). Kennedy signals his restatements by lexical reiteration. Compare line 7 where Kennedy restates his topic sentence, i. e. *whether it will move in the direction of freedom, in the direction of the road that we are taking, or whether it will move in the direction of slavery.* The restatement is signalled by the repetition of the item *whether* and the antonymous pair of stem morphemes *slave : free* in ***free**dom* and ***slave**ry. Whether, freedom* and *slavery* are taking on the signal function of the missing overt plot cue. This example serves to illustrate the important role lexical reiteration plays in addition to its function of establishing coherence, i. e. it signals discourse structure.

At this stage it should be pointed out that we conceive of a reiterated item as forming part of a group and refer to such a group as a LEXICAL CHAIN.[33] We extend this term to include reiteration of key phrases, clauses and sentences, speaking of PHRASAL, CLAUSAL, and SENTENTIAL CHAINS in this connection. The recurrence of these chains helps to ensure coherence in

[31]Cf. Young, Becker, Pike, *op. cit.*, p. 322. The illustrative list takes the following form:

GENERALIZED PLOT	PLOT CUE
B is an instance of A	for example, for instance, e.g.

The generalized plot in this instance could be labelled STATEMENT : EXAMPLES or ASSERTION : INSTANCES.

[32]*Ibid.*, p. 322.

[33]Cf. *ibid.*, pp. 346-348. Cf. also n. 9 above.

discourse. As a result, such recurrences frequently function as cues of discourse structure. Compare ch. 2., exs. 41 and 42, where repetition of the chain *I think it will depend in great measure upon what we do here ...* cues the pattern STATEMENT : CLOSURE BY RETURN.

1.2.3 The Patterns in Discourse

We rename Young, Becker and Pike's generalized plots, calling them PATTERNS IN DISCOURSE or simply DISCOURSE PATTERNS. In accordance with Pilch we enumerate the following discourse patterns:[34]

1) STATEMENT : RESTATEMENT

This pattern "consists in paraphrasing a given proposition either once or several times."[35] In his opening statement Kennedy asserts that the US is not doing enough to maintain freedom in the world and proposes that more must be done, i. e. *Are we doing as much as we can do?* (cf. ch. 2., ex. 19 for our analysis of this section in Kennedy's opening statement). To re-emphasize this point Kennedy restates the proposition twice:

(i) Are we as strong as we should be?
(ii) Are we as strong as we must be?

Overt plot cues for restatement are *in other words, really, in fact* etc.

This general type of restatement can be distinguished from a more specific type of restatement, known as CLOSURE BY RETURN. To end a textual unit or the discourse itself a speaker sometimes summarily restates an idea or statement that occurs in the beginning. In his opening lines Kennedy asserts that freedom in the world depends on what the US does, i. e. *I think it will depend in great measure upon what we do here.* At the end of his opening statement he returns to this idea and closes by giving an almost word for word restatement of his original statement, i. e. *And I think in the final analysis it depends upon what we do here.*

[34]Cf. Herbert Pilch, *Manual of English Phonetics* (München, forthcoming), ch. 6.023. To be noted is the fact that these discourse patterns reflect, to some extent, categories of classical rhetoric, as for example, ANTITHESIS, CONCESSION etc.

[35]*Ibid.*, ch. 6.023 (i).

Pilch extends the pattern statement : restatement to include questions, interpreting the pattern QUESTION : ANSWER as a special case of statement : restatement. The following example from Kennedy's opening statement lends adequacy to the above interpretation:

QUESTION: Are we doing as much as we can do?

ANSWER: I should make it very clear that I do not think we're doing enough.

The QUESTION is merely a *rhetorical*, i. e. FOCALIZING, question (cf. n. 82). Consequently, the ANSWER functions as a simple restatement of the point expressed in the question itself (cf. our analysis in ch. 2., ex. 22 in particular).

2) PROPOSITION : COUNTERPROPOSITION

This pattern "consists in first proposing a generally known 'truth', and then questioning it: 'A is true. Or is it?'"[36] We cite an example from Nixon's opening statement. In lines 125–128 Nixon proposes that the test of a program is how much one spends. In line 140 he questions this PROPOSITION, i. e. *Does this mean that his program is better than ours?*, and then introduces the following COUNTERPROPOSITION:

> The test of a program is not how much money one spends, but what one spends on.

Compare ch. 3, ex. 49 and n. 124 for our discussion of this section.

Pilch extends this pattern to include CONCESSION and ANTITHESIS. CONCESSION can be described by the following paraphrase: "You are right up to a point, but ..."[37] It consists of two parts – the 'actual' CONCESSION followed by a RESERVATION. The *concession* is frequently signalled by such overt plot cues as *you are right, true, I admit, though* and *I concede.* The *reservation* is signalled by the overt plot cues *but, yet, still.* We cite the following example from Kennedy's opening statement: *This is a great country, but I think it could be a greater country.*

In addition to its being a concession, the above example also illustrates an ANTITHESIS. "In antithesis, at least two (syntactically identical) slots are occupied by ANTONYMS ..."[38] The antonymity need not be lexical, but is often

[36] *Ibid.*, ch. 6.023 (ii).

[37] *Ibid.*, ch. 6.023 (ii).

[38] *Ibid.*, ch. 6.023 (ii).

created ad hoc for the given context, as between *great* and *greater* (see ex. above). Like the pattern concession, *antithesis* consists of two parts. Technically, the first part is the THESIS, the second part the ANTITHESIS. Overt plot cues for antithesis are *but* and *not*.

3) GENERAL STATEMENT : EXAMPLES

This pattern consists in first making a general assertion, and then presenting examples to back it up. In lines 42-45 of his opening statement Kennedy asserts that he's dissatisfied with the progress that America has been making. This assertion functions as a GENERAL STATEMENT, which is evidenced by the fact that Kennedy goes on to specify where and how the USA has not made enough progress, i. e. he cites EXAMPLES in support of his general assertion (ll. 49 to 94). Compare ch. 2, ex. 23 for our analysis of this section of Kennedy's opening statement. Overt plot cues for this discourse pattern are *for example, for instance, e. g.*

The DENIAL and REFUTATION of a particular assertion can come in the form of this discourse pattern, namely GENERAL STATEMENT : COUNTER-EXAMPLES. We cite an example from Nixon's opening statement. In line 21 Nixon denies Kennedy's assertion to the effect that the US *has been standing still*. This is equivalent to asserting that the US has 'not' been standing still. To refute Kennedy's assertion (or back his own as it were) Nixon cites an example of where the US has definitely been *moving ahead*, i. e. growth in GNP during the Administration's period of office (ll. 22 to 29).

4) FOCUS[39] : DIGRESSION

DIGRESSION can be defined as the speaker's temporary departure from his topic or, more specifically, as the interruption of a given pattern of discourse by some extraneous element. Kennedy, for example, asserts that he's dissatisfied with America's progress. To back his assertion he cites examples of where America has not made enough progress. In line 77 Kennedy does not merely cite an example, but goes on to point out such past accomplishments of the US as the development of the Tennessee Valley and the construction of the Grand Coulee Dam, i. e. he digresses from his focus or general statement : example pattern (cf. our discussion on p. 48). Overt plot cues for digression are such phrases as *by the way, it might be added.*

---

[39]FOCUS, as we are using the term here, is synonymous to topic, referring to "the point at issue, the subject under discussion, the thrust of the argument." Pilch, *Manual*, ch. 6.025.

A PARENTHESIS, i. e. the insertion of a discrete syntagm into another syntagm,[40] often functions as a digression. In line 11 of his opening statement Nixon inserts the following parenthesis between his concession *we're ahead in this competition* and the reservation *but when you're in a race the only way to stay ahead is to move ahead* – ***As Senator Kennedy I think has implied*** (cf. ch. 3, ex. 8).

5) ENUMERATION : CLIMAX

We distinguish between two types of ENUMERATION – the ENUMERATIVE SERIES and the CLIMACTIC SERIES.

The ENUMERATIVE SERIES consists of constituents from the same semantic field and of the same syntactic construction. These constituents are consecutively stronger in meaning, as *go, run, fly*. The final constituent of the series is the CLIMAX."[41] We cite the following example from Nixon's opening statement, which is an enumeration of the negative attributes Kennedy has ascribed to the Eisenhower Administration:

> Is it true that this Administration ... has been an Administration of **retreat**, of **defeat**, of **stagnation**.

The CLIMACTIC SERIES, unlike the *enumerative series*, is not a series of items from the same semantic field, but rather a series of PROPOSITIONS[42] culminating in a GRAND CONCLUSION (or *climax*). We cite the following climactic series from Nixon's opening statement:

---

[40] Cf. *Ibid.*, ch. 6.023 (iv).

[41] *Ibid.*, ch. 6.023 (iii).

[42] *Webster's*, p. 1168 defines the term PROPOSITION as follows: "In rhetoric, a subject to be discussed or a statement to be upheld." This definition corresponds to our use of the term above. Brooks and Warren distinguish between *proposition* in this sense and a more restricted use of the term, as in 'the proposition of the argument', defining a proposition as "the declaration of a judgement" or "an assertion that may be believed, disbelieved or doubted" and *the* proposition as "the statement of what is to be established by the argument." Brooks and Warren, *op. cit.*, p. 137, p. 8 and p. 137. *The* proposition may be the premise of an argument or the conclusion. Cf. Brooks and Warren, *op. cit.*, pp. 137-151. Cf. also in this connection Young, Becker and Pike, *op. cit.*, pp. 231-233. When we use Brooks and Warren's term *the* proposition we are referring to the CONCLUSION of an argument. Cf. ch. 2, n. 81 and ch. 3, ex. 9. Cf. also Pilch, *Manual*, ch. 6.024.

Let's take schools.
Let's take hydroelectric power.
Let us take hospitals.

The climax in this instance is signalled by intonational means (cf. ch. 3, exs. 28-30).

1.3 The Intonation Model

This section is intended as a short description of the intonational means at the speaker's disposal for signalling discourse structure.[43] The model of English intonation proposed by Pilch[44] serves as the basis for this description. According to Pilch intonation is analyzable as "phonological structure", i. e. it "can be analyzed in terms of an inventory of discrete contrastive elements ('-emes') and of their hierarchy (clusters, groups, etc.)."[45] This mode of analysis is identical to that used for segmental structure, e. g., the monosyllable of English.

1.3.1 The Inventory

The inventory contains four PITCH PATTERNS. These *pitch patterns* can be described in terms of phonological features as follows:

1) the CONVEX MID-FALL /  /

2) the CONVEX LOW FALL /  /

3) the CONCAVE (MID-) FALL /  /

4) the (CONCAVE MID-) RISE /  /

[43] We are focusing on the 'structure' not the 'usage' of intonation.

[44] Cf. Herbert Pilch, "English Intonation as Phonological Structure," *Word*, 31 (1980), pp. 55-67. Cf. also in this connection Pilch, *Manual*, ch. 6.

[45] Pilch, "English Intonation," p. 55.

"All four pitch patterns start at about the same pitch level"[46], i. e. at level /2/. In accordance with Pike[47], we distinguish between the following four *pitch levels*: /1 2 3 4/. In this numbering /1/ is the highest, /4/ the lowest pitch level. Were we to describe the pitch patterns above in conventional terms[48], i. e. with the pitch levels as distinctive, we would obtain the following four groups:

1) /233/
2) /24/
3) /323/
4) /232/

The conventional transcription above helps to elucidate not only the statement made above (i. e. the pitch patterns start at about the same level), but also the following three descriptive statements:[49]

1) the convex low fall descends over a much wider interval than the other three pitch patterns.

2) the concave (mid-) fall usually has a convex rise prefixed to it before it starts to descend.

3) the (concave mid-) rise descends first before rising.

1.3.2 Modifications

These four pitch patterns can be subjected to four kinds of modification: 1) an 'extra-high pitch', 2) a 'fadeaway', 3) 'extra-length', and 4) an 'anticipated high pitch'.

---

[46] *Ibid.*, p. 57.

[47] Kenneth L. Pike, *The Intonation of American English* (Ann Arbor, 1945), pp. 25-26.

[48] Cf. Pilch, "English Intonation," p. 61 on his reasons for not choosing this mode of description.

[49] *Ibid.*, p. 57.

1) The EXTRA-HIGH PITCH (transcribed by the number /1/) is "often accompanied by pharyngeal rasp and/or extra voice volume plus lengthening of the initial consonant."[50]

2) The FADEAWAY (transcribed by the letter /f/) is characterized by pitch drift. The pitch becomes progressively lower and the voice volume progressively weaker and breathier, "often to the point of vocal fry, whisper, even inaudibility."[51]

3) EXTRA-LENGTH (transcribed by a colon /:/) often co-occurs with an extra-high pitch. In our empirical data it is limited to the concave fall and the rise.

4) In the case of the ANTICIPATED HIGH PITCH (transcribed by the letter /a/) "the pitch pattern starts on the usual high level at the end of the proclitic stretch [see below]. Then there is a pitch break, and the pitch continues low on the 'stressed syllable.'"[52]

1.3.3 Contours

The elementary unit of intonation in English is the CONTOUR. It is formed by associative sequences of pitch patterns. The standard contour can be divided into three segments:

1) the NUCLEUS
   - the segment with the most pitch movement, the segment covering the widest pitch interval. This 'wider pitch movement' is at the beginning of the nucleus, i. e. on the first pitch pattern of the nucleus and is "conventionally categorized as 'primary stress', the 'major sentence stress' and the like."[53]

---

[50] *Ibid.*, p. 58.

[51] Pilch, *Manual*, ch. 6.116 (iv).

[52] Pilch, "English Intonation", p. 58. We define PROCLITIC as that stretch of level pitch which is often prefixed to the 'stressed syllable', i. e. the place where the pitch movement proper starts.

[53] Pilch, "English Intonation," p. 59.

2) the PRECONTOUR

- the segment preceding the nucleus. Characteristic for the precontour is its fast speech tempo.

3) the POSTCONTOUR

- the segment following the nucleus. The postcontour is characterized by a "gradual slowdown in speech tempo, often coupled with pitch drift (i. e. lower and lower pitch) and weaker voice."[54]

We transcribe this minimal INTONATION CONTOUR by placing the nucleus in an inner pair of square brackets, the whole contour in an outer pair:

[PRECONTOUR [NUCLEUS] POSTCONTOUR]

Every complete contour must contain a nuclear segment, but not necessarily a precontour or postcontour segment.

The nuclear pitch patterns, as already stated, cover wider pitch intervals. Accordingly, the pitch patterns in the precontour and postcontour cover narrower intervals. For analytical purposes we refer to these precontour and postcontour pitch patterns as allophones of the nuclear pitch patterns, much in the same way as we speak of different allophones of a vowel or consonant.

There is no limit to the number of pitch patterns per contour. Our empirical observations thus far show that the number of pitch patterns in the nucleus, however, is limited to maximally two. The precontour and postcontour can have an indefinite number of pitch patterns. When necessary, the boundary between adjacent pitch patterns is indicated by a downward stroke /|/. We cite the following example from Pilch of a single contour with many pitch patterns (cf. Pilch, "English Intonation," p. 59).

[*particularly, it's just as good* | *if not*
a

better, as, [*any of the Ivy League Schools,*]
a

which are so much more vaunted]
a-

Note the /a/ in the above transcription to indicate an *anticipated high pitch*. The commas in the transcription mark *pauses*. *Pauses* can occur in two places:

[54] *Ibid.*

"1) at the boundaries between pitch patterns ...; and 2) at the boundary between the pitch movement proper and the proclitic prefix, notably at the last syllable preceding the nucleus (as in the example above) ..."[55]

In this connection it should be noted that there is no upper or lower limit to the span of any given pitch pattern or contour. "Contours and pitch patterns extend over an unlimited sequence of segmental and morphological material."[56] They may cover a single word or "long phrases where the boundaries between intonation units often crisscross the syntactic boundaries."[57]

1.3.4 Contour Types

Pilch distinguishes between the following four CONTOUR TYPES of English:

CONTOUR TYPE [1]

The nucleus starts "at the same or a slightly higher pitch level as the preceding precontour pitch pattern," (i. e. at approximately pitch level /2/) "unless either is modified by extra-height or by fadeaway."[58]

CONTOUR TYPE [2]

The nucleus starts "lower than the preceding precontour pitch pattern, and there is neither pause nor proclitic pitch at the boundary between the precontour and the nucleus."[59]

CONTOUR TYPE [3]

In this contour type the pitch pattern in the nucleus is modified by a pitch break. These modified pitch patterns can be regarded as allophones conditioned by contour type.

---

[55] *Ibid.*

[56] *Ibid.*, p. 63.

[57] *Ibid.*

[58] *Ibid.*, p. 60.

[59] *Ibid.*

CONTOUR TYPE [4]

This contour type combines an extra-high nuclear pitch pattern with an extra-low postcontour pitch pattern.[60]

1.3.5 Clusters

Pilch sets up sixteen PITCH CONFIGURATIONS or BINARY CLUSTERS for English intonation. The pitch configuration [ []] is referred to as the elementary configuration. It is used for the lexical intonation of phrases.

1.4 Working Hypothesis

We hypothesize that there is a CO-OCCURRENCE RELATION between intonation and discourse structure: Given intonation patterns serve as cues for given patterns of discourse, helping the listener to understand what the speaker is talking about.

We choose the term *co-occurrence relation* rather than *correlation* because we envisage this relation as a many-many relation, not as a one-to-one relation. The intonational means that the speaker has at his disposal for signalling discourse structure are restricted. The functions of the different intonation patterns will, therefore, necessarily overlap - a recurring intonation pattern may in some instances function as a cue for more than one discourse pattern.

It should be noted that a given discourse pattern is not necessarily always signalled by the intonational cue we have attached to it. A speaker is free to choose his pitch patterns. "Social tradition does make available certain topical devices for shaping discourse (e. g. for answering questions), but

[60]Our description of contour type [4] does not correspond to the description in Pilch, "English Intonation," p. 60. The discrepancy is the result of a change made by Pilch in November 1983.

nobody is constrained to use them just on the 'suitable' occasions."[61] In accordance with the above statement we formulate our working hypothesis:[62]

> Discourse structure is signalled by a set of intonational cues, which the speaker may employ (but need not employ) to help transmit his message.

Should the speaker choose not to employ these intonational cues, however, he may run the risk of producing a piece of discourse which is rhetorically ineffective, if not incoherent, for "it is the exploitation of such devices that ensures the coherence and intelligibility of discourse."[63] Inappropriate intonation, in other words, can convert any well-formed written text into a bad text, i. e. it can evoke the impression of an incoherent text.[64] The semantic cues in a well-formed text, of course, should help the listener to eventually sort out the speaker's message.

---

[61] Herbert Pilch, "Intonation in Discourse Analysis," *Phonetica*, 34 (1977), p. 90.

[62] We formulate our working hypothesis in general terms. The individual hypotheses underlying this general hypothesis (as, for example, rising pitch co-occurs with yes-no questions) are implicitly stated in our empirical data. Cf. the appendix and the individual analyses.

[63] Pilch, "Intonation in Discourse," p. 88.

[64] Cf. *Ibid.*, pp. 81 ff.

2. JOHN F. KENNEDY'S OPENING STATEMENT

John F. Kennedy's opening statement is a perfect example of 'getting to the point'. In the opening lines Kennedy introduces his topic sentence, which could be paraphrased in the following way: The main issue in the 1960 election campaign is whether the world will exist in freedom or slavery. This topic sentence is presented as an antithesis. The 1960 election campaign is contrasted with the 1860 election campaign, where the main issue was not whether the world would exist in freedom or slavery, but rather whether the American nation could exist in freedom or slavery (ll. 1–6).

To introduce focus on this topic Kennedy uses an intonational cue which we regard as topical for introducing focus or indicating a shift in focus: a concave fall on the first lexical item in the precontour. Kennedy's use of this intonational cue deviates from normal usage in so far as he shifts the concave fall to the grammatical word *in*.[65] This enables him to use the lexical item *election* to cue his antithesis. By placing an anticipated high pitch on *election of*, Kennedy signals that the present election, i. e. the election of 1960, is to be compared to some previous election, i. e. to the election of 1860.

Ex. 1 [*In the, election of eighteen* [*sixty*]] (1)[66]
a-

To an American aware of his nation's history it should be self-evident that Kennedy is anticipating the year 1860. 1860 is the only year in the history of the USA in which there was an election campaign with comparable political issues. In the year 1860 the conflict over slavery between the North

[65] The concave fall on the grammatical word *in* could also be interpreted as a cue of restatement, implying that the audience already knows what the issue was in the 1860 election campaign, but is simply being reminded again (cf. the appendix for other instances of pitch patterns on grammatical words to cue a restatement). Both interpretations are equally plausible. It is impossible to give a clear-cut answer as to which interpretation is the 'correct' one. Cf. Herbert Pilch, "Intonation als kommunikative Funktion," in *Festschrift zum 60. Geburtstag von Franz Link*, ed. Ulrich Halfmann, Kurt Müller and Klaus Weiss (Berlin, 1984), 202-204.

[66] The number(s) in round brackets refer(s) to the respective lines in the orthographic transcription of Kennedy's, i. e. Nixon's opening statement.

and the South was threatening to turn into a civil war; in the year 1960 the Cold War was in full swing with its constant threat of leading to actual war.

Looking at the written transcript of these opening lines we notice that the antithesis *election of 1860* vs. *election of 1960* is cued by the plot cues *question was : question is* and *this nation could exist : the world will exist.* In the spoken text these plot cues are accentuated in order to point to their antithetical function. For the sake of clarity we shall refer to the two parts of Kennedy's antithesis as (a) and (b) respectively. In (a) not only the plot cue *question was* but also the plot cue *nation* is given a *precontour stress*[67]; the former a concave fall, the latter a convex fall. An anticipated high pitch on *this* anticipates the plot cue *nation.* In (b) the plot cue functioning antithetically to *question was,* i. e. *question is,* is characterized by a convex fall in the precontour. This convex fall is modified by an extra-high pitch, presumably to emphasize the antithesis. The plot cue functioning antithetically to *nation,* i. e. *world,* receives a concave fall in the nucleus. Its contrastive function is underlined by the extra-length modification on the concave fall.

This distribution of pitch patterns is topical for antithesis. If the speaker uses a 'concave fall plus a convex fall' in the thesis, he will reverse the order of the pitch patterns in the antithesis and vice versa (see ex. 2a and b below). Should the antithesis consist of only one antithetical pair then the concave fall usually contrasts with the convex fall. If the speaker uses a concave fall in the thesis, he will generally use a convex fall in the antithesis, and inversely.[68]

Ex. 2a [*In the, election of eighteen* [*sixty*]]

a-

---

[67] It should be noted that whenever we use the term PRECONTOUR STRESS (i. e. NUCLEAR or POSTCONTOUR STRESS) we are simply referring to the presence of a pitch pattern in precontour (i. e. nuclear or postcontour) position. For a detailed discussion on the notion of STRESS cf. Pilch, *Manual,* ch. 6.013 and ch. 6.117.

[68] Cf. Pilch, "English Intonation," p. 57. This topical usage generally applies for antitheses where the antithetical counterparts are explicitly stated. Where the antithesis is merely implied, however, it is generally signalled by a concave fall. When the concave fall occurs in the nucleus, it is often modified by extra-length; when it occurs in the precontour, it is modified by an extra-high pitch. Cf. ch. 2., ex. 3 and the appendix in this connection.

[2] [*Abraham Lincoln said the question was* |

whether this nation, could ex-[*ist*]]
a

[*half slave, or half* [*free*]] (1-3)

Ex. 2b [3] [*In the election of nineteen* [*sixty*]
a a

and with the world around us]

[*the question is* | *whether the*
1

[*world will exist*]]
:

[3] [*half* [*slave*]]
a

[3] [*or half* [*free*]] (4-6)
a 1

Of further interest in the above transcription of Kennedy's antithesis is his use of contour type [3] to cue the restated lexical items in (b) *sixty, half slave* and *half free*. For other instances of contour type [3] cuing restated lexical items compare the appendix. In this connection it should be mentioned that contour type [2] is also frequently used as a cue for restatement. Accordingly, one could interpret Kennedy's use of contour type [2] on the lexical item *exist* in (a) as a cue signalling that he's merely restating what Abraham Lincoln once said. For further examples see the appendix.

The last point which we note in the above transcription is the concave rise on *half free* in (b). A concave rise in this position is conventionally interpreted as a cue signalling that the speaker has not finished what he wants to say, i. e. it acts as a 'linking device'. We accept this interpretation with the following reservation. Its function as a linking device is subordinate to its function as a cue for *grand conclusion*.[69] The *grand conclusion* in this instance is Kennedy's repetition of the items *half slave* and *half free* to signal the completion of his antithesis. The orotund voice quality as well as the emphatic extra-high pitch accompanying the concave rise lend support to this interpretation.[70] As a linking device, the concave rise signals that Kennedy is going to comment on his antithesis.

Kennedy continues by restating his topic sentence (ll. 7-9), while at the same time emphasizing that *we are taking* the road to freedom (l. 8). *We* refers anaphorically to *this nation*, i. e. the USA. Unlike its referent, however, it has an added dimension of meaning. The inclusive meaning of *we* enables Kennedy to identify himself not only with his audience, but also with the nation as a whole. By using *we* in this collective sense Kennedy creates a feeling of solidarity between himself and his listeners. It is precisely at this moment that Kennedy sets his rhetoric to work. He asserts that freedom in the world *will depend in great measure upon what we do* (ll. 10-11), but at the same time qualifies this assertion as his personal opinion, i. e. *I think*. By shifting from *we* to *I* Kennedy

(a) dissociates himself from what Nixon (or anyone else) might think. The concave fall on *I* modified by an extra-high pitch implies the contrast to *he*, i. e. specifically the contrast to *Nixon thinks*. For further examples of the antithetical use of the concave fall in the precontour when coupled with an extra-high pitch compare the appendix.

Ex. 3 [*I think* | *it will depend* ... (10)
1

In addition to its antithetical function, the concave fall on *I* also introduces focus on Kennedy's assertion.

(b) breaks the *we*-bond between himself and his audience and simultaneously invites the audience to re-establish this bond. The audience must interpret Kennedy's belief, i. e. freedom depends on what the US does, as a reflection of their own belief, if they want to be 'co-we's' in the collective *we do* of line 11. This entails that the audience identifies itself with Kennedy, not Nixon.

[69]This term is adopted from Pilch, *Manual*, ch. 6.023 (iii) and ch. 6.124 (iii).

[70]Cf. *Ibid.*, ch. 6.124 (iii).

(c) sets himself up as the leader of this collective *we*.

Provided that the audience does identify itself with him, Kennedy is now in the position to convince them that a certain course of action must be followed, presumably, under his leadership. What is proposed specifically is an increased effort on the part of the people of the USA, for only then can freedom be maintained (ll. 35-38). This is the major proposition in Kennedy's opening statement (cf. ch. 2., ex. 19). Freedom, then (as Kennedy asserts) depends on what the USA does. This is to be seen in contrast to what the other nations in the world do; more precisely, to what the Soviet and Chinese communists do. This antithetical interpretation may seem a bit far-fetched to the reader of the written transcript. Not so to the listener. Let us recapitulate. In the restatement of his topic sentence Kennedy emphasizes that *we are taking* the road to freedom. Above we said that the sphere of inclusion of *we* is *this nation*, i. e. the USA. The sphere of exclusion of *we*, consequently, are the other nations in the world, alias 'they'. By focusing[71] on the *we* in *we are taking* Kennedy brings out this *we* ≠ *they* contrast. He suggests that 'they' are taking the road to slavery, since the road that *we are taking* is the road to freedom. The nuclear concave fall on *we are taking* modified by extra-length signals this contrast. When modified by extra-length a concave fall in the nucleus frequently cues an antithesis which is not explicitly expressed.[72]

Ex. 4 [*we are taking*] (8)

 :

From the general political context of the year 1960 one can easily infer that the Soviet and Chinese communists are to be understood as the specific 'non-we's'. Kennedy plays on the audience's inclination to associate the words 'freedom' and 'USA' on the one hand, 'slavery' and the 'Soviet Union and China' on the other hand. This is confirmed explicitly in Kennedy's digression in lines 14-24.

In lines 10-11 Kennedy not only reinforces this *we* ≠ *they* contrast, but also introduces the key idea of his opening statement: Freedom in the

[71] Reminder: Our analysis is based on the 'spoken' text not the written transcript. Therefore, we are primarily concerned with the intonational means of achieving focus.

[72] This general rule does not hold once the implied antithesis has been established. Cf. *we do* in ex. 5 below.

world depends on what the USA does, implying that what the Soviet and Chinese communists do works against freedom. The COMPLEX NUCLEUS on *we do* underlines the antithesis to *they do* (cf. ch. 3 and n. 108 for a description of the *complex nucleus*).

Ex. 5 [*I think* | *it will depend in great measure* | *upon*
1

what [*we* *do*] *here in the United States*] (10-11)

In this connection it is noteworthy that the reference item *here* (which refers cataphorically to the USA), and the lexical item *United States* receive a postcontour stress, they 'echo' the nuclear pitch configuration in the reverse order. This type of ECHOING POSTCONTOUR (i. e. a postcontour in which the preceding pitch patterns are echoed in the reverse order), is "a cue for more specific information."[73] The specific information given in this instance indirectly reinforces the *we ≠ they* contrast, *here* and *in the United States* do not function antithetically as such. By focusing on these two items in the postcontour first, Kennedy prepares the listener for his later focus on these key words in the nucleus (cf. ch. 2., exs. 11 and 13). To be noted is the fact that these key words belong to the lexical chain *nation*.

To further underline his *we do ≠ they do* contrast Kennedy follows up his general assertion with two restatements. In these restatements Kennedy puts into concrete terms what is meant by *we do*, introducing two phrasal chains which play an important part in ensuring coherence in his text (cf. ll. 12–13). The first restatement is cued by contour type [2]. The second restatement is an echoing postcontour, in which not only the nucleus, but also the precontour pitch configuration is echoed. In contrast to the echoing postcontour in example 5 (see above), this echoing postcontour echoes the preceding pitch pattern configuration in the identical order. This type of *echoing postcontour* is "a cue for restatement with or without supplementary information."[74] Note that the echoing postcontour echoes either only the nuclear pitch configuration or both the precontour and nuclear pitch configuration.

---

[73]Herbert Pilch, *Ms. 2*, p. 153.

[74]Pilch, *Manual*, ch. 6.227.

Ex. 6 [2] [*on the kind of society that* [*we build*] (12)

Ex. 7 *on the kind of strength that we maintain*] (13)

Up to this point we have concentrated on the first thirteen lines of our text. These thirteen lines function as a unit, as the introduction to Kennedy's opening statement. In this section Kennedy introduces two key phrases, which are crucial in ensuring coherence in his opening statement. These key phrases are:

(1) the question is

(2) I think it will depend in great measure upon what we do here in the United States

The first key phrase recurs in a modified form in line 33 and 143; the second key phrase, also in modified form, recurs in lines 128–129 and 146–147.

In line 14 Kennedy digresses from his main topic, shifting his focus to the communists and what they are doing. This digression is important in so far, as it confirms what has only been suggested thus far, i. e. the antithetical relation between the US and the two major communist countries. Seen in relation to the previous section, Kennedy is merely elaborating on a sub-topic already alluded to in line 8 and 10. What is noteworthy is how Kennedy accomplishes the shift in focus to this sub-topic. He takes up the lexical item *we*, uses the intonational cue for indicating a shift in focus, i. e. a concave fall in the precontour, and modifies this intonational cue by the feature extra-length.

Ex. 8 [*We discuss tonight, do-*[*mestic issues*]] (14)
: a

This renewed stress on *we* is primarily what captures our attention. Contrary to prior observations, however, the *we* in this instance does not seem to function contrastively. This is due to two factors:

(1) In the preceding section our analysis of *we* was restricted to its use in the nucleus. In nuclear position *we* functioned contrastively when coupled with a concave fall modified by extra-length. This does not seem to be the case in the precontour. For instances of the antithetical use of *we* in the precontour compare the appendix.

(2) More important, however, is the fact that the *we* in line 14 does not have the same referent as the *we* in line 8 and 11, it refers not to *this nation*, but to the two speakers in the debate, Nixon and Kennedy. Therefore, what has been said above cannot hold in this instance. Here, Kennedy uses the word *we* to characterize the immediate situation; in other words, to indicate that Nixon and he himself, as the major participants in the ensuing debate, are going to discuss *domestic issues*. From the applause perceptible on the tape, I assume that Nixon and Kennedy are debating in front of an audience. Therefore, even if *we* also refers to potential participants from the rows of the audience, it certainly does not refer to the nation as a whole.

Let us summarize. Kennedy uses *we* in combination with the lexical items *discuss tonight* to focus our attention on the immediate situation. By coupling these words with the appropriate intonational cue, Kennedy indicates his intention of changing the topic. Instrumental in actually bringing about a transition from the main topic to the sub-topic is the reservation Kennedy attaches to his concession: Domestic issues must be seen in the light of international issues (ll. 14-17). The concession in its complete form could be paraphrased as follows:

> Granted, we are concerned with domestic issues in this debate, but domestic issues stand in a direct relation to international affairs, i. e. to our relationship with the Soviet communists in particular.

This concession is cued by a concave fall on the lexical items *domestic issues* (cf. ex. 8 above).

Although the Soviet communists are presented as posing the major threat to world peace, the Chinese communists - it is implied - can gradually be regarded as posing an almost equal threat to world peace. To establish focus on this topic, i. e. the Chinese communist threat, Kennedy uses the topical intonational cue on the lexical items *the Chinese communists* and continues by stating the following generally known 'truth': *The Chinese communists have always had a large population* (ll. 21-22).[75] This generally known 'truth' functions as a concession. This is confirmed by the concave fall on

[75]By anticipating *population* as the focus of *large*, i. e. by placing an anticipated high pitch on the proclitic syllable of *population*, Kennedy underlines that this fact is common knowledge - that the Chinese *have always had a large population*.

population and the overt plot cue following *population*, i. e. *but*. The precontour stress on *always* signals that this word functions contrastively.

Ex. 9 [*The Chinese communists* | *have always had* | *a*
1

large popu-[*lation*]] (21-22)
a

In the reservation to his concession, Kennedy supplies the lexical item *now* to act as the antithetical counterpart of *always*. I use the word 'act' to indicate that *now* and *always* are antonyms *ad hoc*, at least overtly. The lexical antithesis which underlies the ad hoc antithesis as expressed by Kennedy in his concession contains the lexical antonyms *always* vs. *never* and *then* vs. *now*. This lexical antithesis can be paraphrased as follows:

> Even though the Chinese communists have *always* had a large population, they were *never* important or dangerous in the past.
> In contrast to *then*, however, the Chinese communists are *now* important and dangerous.

Ex. 10 [3] [*but they are important* | *and*

dangerous [*now*]] (22)
a :

To be noted is the nuclear concave rise on *now* signalling the antithesis, instead of the topical concave fall (cf. ch. 2., exs. 2a and 2b). The orotund voice quality accompanying the concave rise indicates that the antithesis functions as a grand conclusion. This function is superimposed upon the antithetical function performed by *now*. The simultaneous linking function that the concave rise performs is subordinate to its function as a cue for grand conclusion (cf. ch. 2., ex. 2b).

This sub-topic, i. e. the Soviet and Chinese communist threat, extends to line 24, where Kennedy resumes his main topic. He does not give an overt plot cue to signal the transition, but merely sets in with a modified version of the phrasal chain *on the kind of society* ... (l. 12), i. e. *the kind of country* ... The lexical item *country* links the preceding section with what follows, it does not, however, signal the shift of focus back to the main topic. The listener is not immediately aware of the fact that *country* figures as an element in the lexical chain *USA, this nation* etc., i. e. that it refers to the *USA* and not to *China*, as in the preceding section. It is the postmodifier of *country*, i. e. *we have here*, which functions as the actual cue for the shift of focus back to the USA and thereby back to the main topic. The nuclear stress on *here* makes explicit which country Kennedy is talking about, it confirms that the deictic reference is, in fact, to the USA. The syntactically parallel restatements following (ll. 26 and 27; exs. 12 and 13 below) act as further confirmation.

Ex. 11 [2] [*The kind of country* | *we have* [*here*]] (25)

Ex. 12 [2] [*The kind of society* | [*we have*]] (26)

Ex. 13 [2] [*The kind of strength* | *we build* |

in the United [*States*]...] (27) 1

Kennedy's shift of focus back to his main topic, as a whole, is rhetorically ineffective. He does not use an intonational cue which clearly marks the shift in focus, such as *contrastive nuclear stress*[76] on *here* to underline the antithesis *their country* (China) vs. *our country (USA)*. Instead, he uses a cue which barely marks the transition. The nucleus on *here* is low in contrast to the high forceful precontour (the distinguishing characteristic of contour type [2]) and, as such, cues an ABSENCE OF FOCUS (cf. ch. 3 and n. 117). This ineffective transition can be explained in either of two ways:

1) as a weak point in Kennedy's opening statement, i. e. as unintentional; or
2) as intentional.

[76] A concave fall modified by extra-length would have been a means of signalling *contrastive nuclear stress* in this position (cf. ex. 4 above where Kennedy signals the implicit antithesis *we ≠ they* in this way). It should be noted that unless otherwise specified, we are always referring to contour type [1] when making descriptive statements of this kind.

I choose the second interpretation. Kennedy uses the topical intonational cue for restatement on the two phrasal chains which follow (i. e. contour type [2]), and places a concave rise on the last element in the second restatement (i. e. on *States*) to act as a link between the last phrasal chain of the series and the comment *will be the defense of freedom.* The extra-high pitch modification on the concave rise raises our expectations that Kennedy is now going to present the new point in his discussion, in spite of any initial difficulties he might have had in establishing focus. The subsequent total *absence of focus* on this comment, i. e. the BACKGROUNDING of the comment cued by the postcontour position and fadeaway,

Ex. 14] *will be the defense of freedom*] (28)

indicates that Kennedy is not trying to make a point, but that he is merely restating his general proposition of lines 10–11 in more specific terms. The shift in precontour stress to the lexical item *kind* in the phrasal chains above (ex. 11, 12 and 13 above; cf. also ex. 6 and 7 above) signals that they function as restatements of the phrasal chains in lines 12 and 13, that they are a mere enumeration of the foregoing specification. This could account for the general absence of focus on the first phrasal chain of this series, i. e. on *the kind of country we have here.*

In support of this interpretation we call the reader's attention to Kennedy's choice of precontour pitch patterns for *the kind of country, the kind of society, the kind of strength.* The choice does not seem to have been a random choice, the order of occurrence of the precontour pitch patterns is identical to that topically used on enumerative series, i. e.

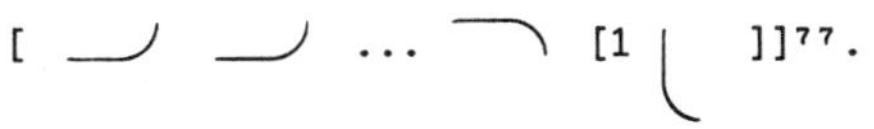

The difference is only in the distribution of these pitch patterns. Kennedy does not stay within the boundaries of the intonation contour, and he restricts their use to the precontour. Bearing this in mind, I would interpret the pitch pattern configuration on *kind of country, kind of society* and *kind of strength* as a variant of the enumerative configuration. *Kind of country, kind of society* and *kind of strength*, accordingly, could be interpreted as an enumerative series. The subsequent backgrounding of the comment lends sup-

[77] Cf. Pilch, *Manual*, ch. 6.226.

port to our interpretation. The backgrounded comment adds emphasis to the last phrasal chain of the series and as such fulfills the same function as the extra-high pitch modification on the low convex fall in the enumerative series. Compare examples 19, 20 and 21 below in this connection. They follow the same pattern.

In line 29 Kennedy finally presents his new topic. He takes up his general proposition of lines 10-11 and elaborates on it, making freedom in the world dependent on if America does *well*, i. e. *If we do well here ... then I think freedom will be secure around the world.* This particular assertion can be interpreted as an APODICTIC STATEMENT - a statement which claims to be necessarily true, i. e. a statement which rules out contradiction. The conditional clause *if ... then* is to be understood in the following way: Freedom in the world will be maintained *if and only if* America does well. The qualification *I think* in the *then*-clause does not qualify Kennedy's assertion as such, it merely softens the severity of his statement. It is only an "'apparent qualification'".[78] The justification for the above interpretation is the intonation Kennedy uses. Kennedy uses contour type [4] instead of (the neutral) contour type [1] to underline the *if*-clause, and backgrounds the *then*-clause.

Ex. 15 [4] [*If* [*we do* | *well*] *here*] ...] *then I*

think | *freedom will be secure around*

the world] (29-31)
a f

The extra-high nucleus on *we do well* emphasizes the condition that freedom in the world will only be guaranteed if the USA does *well*. By echoing the nuclear pitch configuration of the proposition in lines 10-11 (see ex. 5 above), Kennedy further underlines that it is imperative that the USA (*we*) *do well*. The extra-low (but at the same time quite forceful) postcontour simultaneously backgrounds and re-emphasizes the specification *here*.

The backgrounding of *then I think freedom will be secure around the world* (postcontour position and fadeaway) indicates that this *then*-clause functions as a mere restated comment (cf. ex. 14 above).

[78]Cf. *Ibid.*, ch. 6.024.

The two *if*-clauses preceding the *then*-clause (ll. 29-30) can be interpreted as restatements of *if we do well here* cued by contour type [2]. In these restatements Kennedy introduces the lexical chains *meet our obligations* and *move ahead*, which play an important part in ensuring coherence in his opening statement (cf. ll. 100-101 and ll. 124-125).

Ex. 16 [2] [*if we meet our obli-* [*gations*]] (29)
1

Ex. 17 [2] [*if we're moving a-* [*head*]] (29-30)
a

Doing well is to be equated with *doing more/better.*[79] This is to be inferred not only from the compound verb *move ahead*, but also from the syllogism underlying Kennedy's argument:[80]

Major Premise: We want to do enough to maintain freedom.
Minor Premise: It's not enough what we're doing at present.
Conclusion: Therefore, we must do more.

Kennedy's argument itself could be restated as follows:

If freedom is to be maintained, we must do more/better.
Conversely:
If we do more/better, then freedom will be maintained.

The proposition[81] of the argument is presented in the form of a *rhetorical* or FOCALIZING QUESTION[82] as we choose to call it (ll. 35-38). The overt plot

---

[79]The 'echo' of *Piers Plowman* is presumably unintentional.

[80]For a discussion on syllogisms compare Young, Becker and Pike, *op. cit.*, pp. 231-233.

[81]Cf. n. 42.

[82]By using the term FOCALIZING QUESTION we avoid any misunderstandings which might arise as a result of different interpretations of what is or isn't to be considered a *rhetorical question*. We define a *focalizing question* as a question asked strictly for rhetorical effect, it is a more emphatic way of introducing a topic than the equivalent statement form. The answer is predetermined by the semantic and pragmatic context. For this reason we interpret the answer, if it is explicitly stated, as a restate-

cue *therefore* (*therefore* implies arguing from a premise)[83] coupled with the appropriate intonational cue for introducing focus directs our attention to this essential point of the argument. As already stated, *the* proposition takes the form of a focalizing question. To pave the way for this focalizing question, Kennedy expressly announces he is posing a question:

Ex. 18 [3] [*Therefore* | *I think the question before the* a *American people* [*is*]] (33-34)

The key phrase *the question is* creates a chain link between this newly-begun section and the first section. Note the anticipated high pitch on *question* and the use of contour type [3] to cue the restatement.

In the focalizing question *we do* from line 11 is taken up again, also creating a link. In contrast to the *we do* in line 11, however, the present progressive form of *do* is used here. This suggests an antithesis between what is being done at present and what could be done (if the US did better). The nuclear stress on the modal auxiliary *can* confirms that a contrast is intended. Cf. the appendix in this connection.

Ex. 19 [*Are we doing* | *as much as we* [*can do*]][84] (35)

The restatement of the focalizing question – itself in the form of a focalizing question – follows the same pattern: *How strong we are* is to be understood as antithetical to *how strong we should* and *must be*.

---

ment and not as a genuine answer. It merely re-emphasizes the point being expressed in the question itself.

[83] Cf. Halliday and Hasan, *op. cit.*, p. 257.

[84] It is a widespread opinion that questions of the type in examples 19-21 - called *yes-no* questions "because the answer (which may be expressed or just implied) is *yes* or *no*" (Geoffrey Leech and Jan Svartvik, *A Communicative Grammar of English* (London, 1975), p. 283, § 778) - usually have a rising pitch pattern in the nucleus. Our empirical observations show that this general rule does not hold for *yes-no* questions when they function as focalizing questions.

Ex. 20 [2] [*Are we as strong* | *as we* [*should be*]] (36)

Ex. 21 [2] [*Are we as strong* | *as we* [*must be*]] (37)

Summing up, it could be said that Kennedy is making the following point in his focalizing question:

> ***What is*** is not ***what ought to be***. Therefore, it is necessary to *do more* in order to attain this *ought to be*.

This is the conclusion that must be drawn, Kennedy's proposition. It is a call for action or 'proposition of action'[85], an appeal to the people of the United States to rally for united action.

Kennedy supports his general proposition by citing instances of where the US is supposedly not doing enough to maintain freedom. He backs these instances by pointing to certain facts. As a result, both his general proposition and the particular instances gain credibility. To direct our attention to this new section with its series of examples (ll. 49-94), Kennedy once again uses the intonational cue for introducing focus.

Ex. 22 [2] [*I should make it very clear* | *that I do*

[*not think*] *we're doing enough*] (42-43)

The nuclear stress on *not think*[86] serves two purposes:

(1) it focuses on Kennedy's opinion, and
(2) it indicates that Kennedy is restating the minor premise of his syllogism (see above).

[85]Cf. Brooks and Warren, *op. cit.*, p. 139.

[86]*Think* is a verb taking transferred negation. Cf. Leech and Svartvik, *op. cit.*, p. 248, § 636. In terms of meaning, *not* belongs to a *that*-clause (*I do not think we're doing enough* = *I think we're not doing enough*). Consequently, nuclear stress on *not think* could be interpreted as being equivalent to: [2] [*I think we're* [*not doing enough*]].

It may not be evident to the reader why I interpret line 42 as a restatement of the minor premise, and not as the minor premise itself. The assertion in line 42 functions as the answer to the three focalizing questions asked in lines 35–38. Focalizing questions, as we have already indicated, are questions asked only for rhetorical effect, to introduce a topic. Thus, in asking these questions, Kennedy has already stated his minor premise. In line 42 he is merely taking up this topic again and explicitly restating that he is convinced that America could do better. If Kennedy were, in fact, presenting his minor premise as *new* information and not as *given* information[87], the quantifier pronoun *enough* would be given the nuclear stress. This analysis corresponds to that of M. A. K. Halliday.

Halliday considers spoken English to be made up of a succession of *tone groups* (i. e. intonation contours)[88], each tone group being a *unit of information*. One part is selected as prominent within each tone group – the *tonic* (i. e. nucleus). According to Halliday, the "function of the tonic is to form the focus of the information: to express what the speaker decides to make the main point or burden of his message."[89] This is precisely what is considered to be *new* information:

> "The information which the speaker decides is to form the focus of the message we may call *new*. The 'new' information is that part of the information unit (it may be the whole of it) which the speaker has decided to present as not being already available to the hearer; that is, as something the hearer could not have supplied for himself. It may be something that has not been mentioned before, or is unexpected, or contrary to what has been implied, and so on."[90]

---

[87]Cf. M. A. K. Halliday, *A Course in Spoken English: Intonation* (Oxford, 1970), p. 40. For the notion of *new* vs. *given* information cf. also Halliday and Hasan, *op. cit.*, p. 27 and pp. 325-326, where they speak of *comment* and *topic*; and Wolfgang Dressler, *Einführung in die Textlinguistik* (Tübingen, 1972), pp. 53-55, where he speaks of *rheme* vs. *theme*.

[88]Compare our description of the intonation contour in section 1.3.3. Our intonation contour differs from Halliday's tone group in so far as it may be followed by a postcontour. Halliday's tone group consists of a *tonic* or *tonic segment*, which may or may not be preceded by a *pretonic* (or *pretonic segment*). Cf. Halliday, *op. cit.*, pp. 1-23.

[89]*Ibid.*, p. 40.

[90]*Ibid.*

The part of the information unit which is not 'new' and does not carry the tonic is referred to as *given*. It is the information which is already known or assumed.

Reverting to example 22 above, it should now be obvious to the reader why we interpreted this unit of information as we did. This interpretation, of course, presupposes that nuclear stress on the negative item *not* can serve as a cue of restatement. Empirical observations verify this claim. To be noted is the simultaneous use of contour type [2] to signal the restatement.

In conclusion, we'd like to mention one more point concerning the above example. By emphasizing the fact that he believes that America is *not doing enough*, Kennedy makes his audience expect some elaboration on this topic. In fact, Kennedy supports his general proposition of action, i. e. *we must do more*, by citing examples of *how* and *where the United States is not doing enough* (see above). Example 22 cues that such examples are to be given, it serves as the general statement in the discourse pattern general statement : examples.

To indicate that he's giving an example, Kennedy does not use a conventional plot cue such as *for example*. Instead, he introduces the phrasal chain *I'm not satisfied*, which acts as a cue for each successive example. This phrasal chain is introduced in line 43.

Ex. 23 [*... that I am not satisfied ...* (43)

Here again, Kennedy emphasizes the fact that it is his own personal dissatisfaction which is the determining factor in coming to the conclusion that America is not making enough progress - the precontour stress on *not satisfied*.

By specifying more exactly the scope of this gradable word *not satisfied*[91], i. e. *as an American*, Kennedy re-establishes the bond between himself and his countrymen.

Ex. 24 [2] [*... that I am not satisfied as an* [*American*]

with the progress that we're making] (43-44)

[91] *As* specifies the role which the gradable word *not satisfied* implies. Cf. Leech and Svartvik, *op. cit.*, p. 103, § 227.

The nucleus on *American* re-focuses on the inclusive *we*. The point Kennedy is suggesting is: Every true American must be dissatisfied with the small amount of progress that's being made. Therefore, the audience must interpret Kennedy's dissatisfaction as a reflection of their own dissatisfaction, if they are true fellow Americans.

To head off any possible objections which might be presented against his assertion, Kennedy concedes that the USA is, in fact, *a great country*. The point at issue, however, he claims, is the fact that it could be an even *greater country*, i. e. again the distinction between *do well* and *do better*. The antithesis *great* vs. *greater* is signalled by the convex vs. the concave fall. Note the concave fall on *country* to cue the concession. Contour type [3] cues the restated lexical items *country* and *greater*.

Ex. 25a [3] [*This is a great* [*country*]] (45)

Ex. 25b [3] [*but I think it could be a* [*greater*]
a

country] (45-46)

Kennedy immediately follows up his concession with a restatement. In the restated concession the nucleus is shifted forward to *powerful*. This is a means of re-emphasizing *great country*, of indicating that *powerful country* functions as a restatement. Contour type [2] functions as a further cue. In the restated reservation the nucleus on *powerful* is anticipated. *More*, as a rule, is not given nuclear stress when expressing a comparison.[92] Note again contour type [3] cuing the restated lexical item *powerful*.

Ex. 26a [2] [*And this is a* [*powerful country*]] (47)
:

Ex. 26b [3] [*but I think it could be* | *a*
a-

more [*powerful* | *country*]] (47-48)
a

[92]Cf. Jürgen Esser, *Englische Prosodie: Eine Einführung* (Tübingen, 1979), p. 57 and p. 89.

Having defended his position against these possible objections, Kennedy finally presents his facts. As stated, the overt cue for each example is the phrasal chain *I'm not satisfied.* This phrasal chain always occurs in the precontour. In the opening example (l. 49) it is characterized by a concave fall on *I'm* and a concave rise beginning on *satisfied* and extending to the end of *to have.* In the subsequent examples (ll. 51, 57, 66, 68, 72, 75, 85) only the lexical item *satisfied* is given a precontour stress. In all but the closing example (l. 85) this precontour stress is a concave rise modified by an anticipated high pitch on *I'm.* With the exception of the example in line 51 the concave rise undergoes the additional modification of extra-length. In the closing example *satisfied* is characterized by an extra-low convex fall plus the anticipated high pitch modification on *I'm.* Compare the appendix page 142.

The sequence of pitch patterns used on the overt plot cue *I'm not satisfied* (or to be more specific, the sequence used on the element *satisfied*) bears a striking resemblance to the sequence topically used for an enumeration (cf. exs. 11, 12 and 13 above and n. 77). Apart from the missing concave fall, the sequences prove to be identical. In a premature closure by return (ll. 83-84), Kennedy supplies the missing link: A concave fall on *these are all the things* signals that one more instance of dissatisfaction is to be added to complete the list of examples.

Ex. 27 [3] [*These are all the things* | *I think in this*
:

country that can make, our society [*strong*]
:

or can mean that it stands still] (83-84)
a

This closure by return is cued not only by the demonstrative pronoun *these,* which refers anaphorically to the examples given from lines 49-82, but also by the repetition of the lexical item *strong* (cf. ll. 36-37) and the introduction of its ad hoc antonym *stand still.* An intonational cue for the closure by return is contour type [3]. The concave rise on *strong* signals both the antithesis and a grand conclusion (see ex. 10 above).

The examples are frequently followed by digressions:

(a) Kennedy backs his particular assertion with an adverbial *because*-clause, expressing the reason why a low rate of economic growth is undesirable (ll. 53-56).

(b) Kennedy specifies his particular assertion by offering as proof what he himself has witnessed (ll. 61-65).

(c) Kennedy follows up his assertion by proposing a general political principle (ll. 70-71).

(d) Kennedy specifies where the US is *failing to develop its natural resources to the fullest*: in the area of hydro-power production. This particular instance is preceded by a digression on past accomplishments, landmarks in the development of the USA (ll. 77-82). This comparison between what has been achieved in the past and what is being achieved at present seems to give rise to the following question: Has the US lost its potential for great achievements? The claim, of course, is that the USA is indeed capable of *doing better*. What the country needs in order to *do better* is a better president.

(e) Kennedy specifies in which ways black Americans do not enjoy their *full constitutional rights* (ll. 86-95).

In each instance the listener is given an intonational cue, indicating where the example ends and the digression begins. The intonational cue is a concave rise on the final item(s) of each example, with the exception of the closing example. In the closing example (ll. 85-86) Kennedy employs a convex fall to mark the boundary between example and digression (cf. the appendix pp. 142-143).

This brief description of the intonational characteristics of Kennedy's examples is sufficient for our purposes. If an example or the digression proves to be of special interest for further analysis, it will be taken up in the appendix. We have just given our reader a cue that we wish to conclude our discussion on the examples Kennedy has cited, namely *is sufficient for our purposes*. Likewise, Kennedy must give his audience some type of transitional cue indicating that he is about to change his topic. He closes by returning to his original proposition, i. e. *we must do more*, which he restates as follows:

Ex. 28 [3] [*I think* | *we can do* [*better*]] (95)

a

Kennedy anticipates the nucleus on *better* by using an anticipated high pitch on *do*, instead of the concave fall precontour customary in topical usage, i. e. LEVEL STRESS on this verbal group:[93]

... do [better].

This has the effect of foregrounding *better* and stressing once more the idea that the USA is capable of *doing better. Level stress* would have made it appear as if this information were being presented as 'new' information and not 'given' information.[94]

The new topic is presented as a proposition followed by a counterproposition. Kennedy insinuates that his political opponents hold the view that he and his fellow Democrats propose the following course of action: *Let's turn everything over to the government*, i. e. the Democrats are in favor of *big government*. Note the use of the echoing postcontour to reduce this proposition to the status of a mere restatement.

Ex. 29 [*I* [*know that there are those* | *who say that*]
:

we want to turn everything over to the

government] (97-98)

The shift in focus to this new topic is marked not only by the concave fall on *know* and *we*, but also by the apparent change in the referent of *we*. The *we* above refers to the political group Kennedy identifies himself with, i. e. the Democratic Party. Provided that there is some truth in what people are saying, one assertion is definitely false – the assertion that Kennedy advocates this course of action. This is confirmed by Kennedy's downright denial in the following line, i. e. *I don't at all.*

Ex. 30 [2] [*I don't* | *at all*] (99)

---

[93]Cf. *dig deeper* in Herbert Pilch, *MS. 1*, p. 91.

[94]Cf. Esser, *op. cit.*, pp. 69-74 and p. 77 on the notion of *level stress*.

It should be noted that both the complex nucleus above and in example 29 function as cues for refutation.[95] In ex. 29 the complex nucleus on *know that there are those who say that* signals that Kennedy is going to refute what some people are saying, i. e. that the Democrats are in favor of *big government.* This cue is reinforced by the echoing postcontour. It is obvious from Kennedy's subsequent denial that he does not want to exclude the possibility that some Democrats may, in fact, be in favor of *big government.* By focusing on his personal standpoint, Kennedy can emphasize the fact that he himself does not belong to this particular group of Democrats.

In general, Kennedy's denial is not very effective. The simultaneous use of contour type [2] cues that it functions as a qualified restatement of the implicit denial in ex. 29 above, i. e. *I* instead of *we do not want to turn everything over to the government.*

In lines 100–102 Kennedy presents his counterproposition. This counterproposition is presented as a concession. Kennedy grants that the *individuals* and *states* should have their autonomous sphere of action, with the following reservation: Governmental intervention is at times necessary. The actual concession is cued by a concave fall in the nucleus. To indicate that this concession also functions as a counterproposition, Kennedy uses the topical intonational cue for a counterproposition, i. e. [[ ]].[96] This pitch configuration is referred to as the FALL-PLUS-RISE[97] by the British school. Note the shift in nuclear stress to *their* in the repetition of the lexical chain *meet their responsibilities* and the use of contour type [3] to cue the restated lexical chain.

Ex. 31 [*I want the individuals to meet their*
a

responsi- [*bilities*]] (100)

Ex. 32 [3] [*And I want the states* | *to meet*
1

[*their responsibilities*]] (101)

---

[95]Compare ch. 3 and n. 108 for a detailed description of the *complex nucleus.*

[96]Cf. Pilch, *Manual,* ch. 6.222.

[97]Cf. Quirk, *et al., op. cit.,* p. 1046.

The reservation to the concession above does not follow the same pattern, even though it is, strictly speaking, also part of the counterproposition.

Ex. 33 [*but I think there is also a* [*national*
a

responsibility]] (102)

To justify such governmental action, Kennedy cites one instance of sensible intervention in the past, i. e. to help develop the Tennessee Valley (In 1933 a Federal Corporation was organized for this purpose – The Tennessee Valley Authority).

Ex.34a [*The people of the United States, individually* |
a a

could [*not have developed the Tennessee Valley*]]
a

Ex.34b [*collectively they* [*could have*]] (105-107)
1

The foregrounded[98] lexical item *individually* (a link in the lexical chain *national responsibility* vs. *individual responsibility*) serves as the overt plot cue signalling that Kennedy is going to comment on *governmental action* vs. *individual action*. The anticipated high pitch modification as well as the pause directly preceding this word underlines its signal value. Bearing Kennedy's concession in mind, it should be evident that he is out to defend *governmental action*. His subsequent comment on *individually* confirms this. In pointing out an area where *individual action* would not have been expedient, it follows that *governmental action* must have been. This is 'quasi'-confirmed by the antithesis *collectively they could have*. I say *quasi*-confirmed because this antithesis does not, in reality, confirm the fact that the development of the Tennessee Valley was the result of a joint effort. On the contrary, the antithesis distorts the fact. By using *could have* (and not *did*), Kennedy merely insinuates that it would have been possible to develop the Tennessee

[98] Cf. ch. 1.2.1. in this connection. The intonational cue for foregrounding is a concave fall.

Valley had there been a joint effort. This false rendering of the facts has a perplexing effect on the listener. As a result, I would interpret this section of Kennedy's opening statement as a weak point in his presentation. *Could have*, it is true, preserves the syntactic parallelism between the thesis and the antithesis (*could not have* vs. *could have*) – but this, in my opinion, is not justification enough for such a blatant distortion of the facts.

This example justifying governmental action in the past is followed by two examples justifying governmental action now (at the time of speaking). The government a) protects the individual from 'big business' interests (ll. 108–112), ex. 35 below); and b) provides for social justice. Effective governmental programs compensate for the shortcomings of individual action (ll. 113–117, ex. 36 below). These examples of sensible governmental intervention now can be interpreted as restatements of the preceding example. I base my interpretation on the following intonational characteristics:

In the first example Kennedy uses contour type [2] to cue the restated thesis and a combination of the same with the echoing postcontour to cue the restated antithesis. The antithetical counterpart of *cannot protect himself*, i. e. *do so*, is shifted to the postcontour in order to foreground the lexical chain *effective governmental programs*, which is taken up in line 117, i. e. *social security system*, and in the closure by return in line 119, i. e. *effective governmental action*. The antithesis as a whole is cued by the topical cues (cf. ch. 2., exs. 2a and 2b in this connection). The concave rise on *protect himself* and *market place* functions as a cue for grand conclusion.

Ex.35a [2] [*he cannot pro-* [*tect himself*] *against*
1

the, forces of | *supply and demand in*

the market place] (109-111)

Ex.35b [2] [*but working together* | *in ef-* [*fective*
1

governmental programs] *he can do so*] (111-112)

In the second example Kennedy uses contour type [3] to cue the restated thesis, or to be more precise, to cue the restated lexical item *individually* from line 105. In the antithesis Kennedy shifts the nucleus to *system* and places an anticipated high pitch on the restated lexical item *social security* (cf. l. 114). The antithetical counterparts are signalled by the concave fall and the concave rise in the thesis vs. the two convex falls in the antithesis.

Ex.36a [3] [*they're not able* | *to sustain themselves* |

indi- [*vidually*]] (115-116)
a

Ex.36b [3] [*but they can sustain themselves* | *through*

the social security [*system*]] (116-117)
a

Kennedy closes this set of examples (ll. 105-117) by returning to his concession in lines 101-102 (see above). This closure by return is presented as an antithesis between *big government* and *effective governmental action*, *big* and *effective* functioning as antonyms ad hoc. To be noted is the pitch configuration Kennedy uses on the concession itself. It signals that the concession also functions as a restated counterproposition.[99] Note also the use of contour type [3] and the anticipated high pitch to cue the closure by return.

Ex.37a [3] [*I don't* | *believe in* [*big government*]] (118)
a :

Ex.37b [2] [*but I believe in effective governmental*
a

[*action*]] (118-119)

Effective governmental action, then, not total governmental control, seems to be the key to a functioning society, a necessary condition for making the American nation a *greater* nation and ensuring that *freedom is maintained* (ll. 120-122). In order to reach this goal, however, it is also essential

[99] Cf. above for the original counterproposition.

for each and every individual to do his share, *to meet his responsibilities* (This is our paraphrase of the lexical chain introduced in l. 29). This insight is the basis for Kennedy's appeal to his fellow countrymen, which is taken up again at this point in an almost word-for-word restatement of the closure by return in line 95.

Ex. 38 [3] [*I think* | *we can do a better* [*job*]] (123)
a

For rhetorical purposes, the new item in this restated closure by return, i. e. *job*, is given full emphasis. The precontour stress, which would normally fall on the item *better*, i. e. level stress, is omitted for the same reasons as in example 28 (above). Nuclear stress on *better* would be contrastive, a function not called for in this instance.

This proposition of action is given added force in lines 123–126. Not doing *a better job* is equated with shirking one's responsibility as an American, a responsibility imposed upon the nation as a whole by the course of events. Note Kennedy's use of contour type [4] again to cue the apodictic statement *I think we're going to have to do a better job, if we are going to meet the responsibilities which time and events have placed upon us.* The extra-high nucleus on *have to do* stresses the fact that doing a better job is no longer a matter of choice, but an obligation which must be fulfilled. The extra-low postcontour re-emphasizes *a better job.*

Ex. 39 [4] [*I think we're going* | *to* [*have to do*]
1

a better job] (123-124)

[*if we are going to meet the responsibilities* |
1 a

which [*time and events*] *have placed upon* us] (124-126)
f

Repetition of the lexical chain *meet one's responsibility*, i. e. *meet the responsibilities*, serves as a link to the preceding section, integrating the topic *individual responsibility* vs. *governmental responsibility* into the text as a whole. Its function is to point out that there is a collective responsibility above and beyond individual and governmental responsibility: All Americans must unite in concerted action to ensure that freedom is maintained, it is their obligation to do so (ll. 123–126).

This idea of a joint obligation is put into more concrete terms in lines 130–142. The USA must regain the respect of the world by proving its superiority to the Soviet and Chinese communists. Under the guidance of such an exemplary president as Franklin D. Roosevelt, the USA was once in the position of having Latin America look up to it, not to the Soviet and Chinese communists. Under the guidance of an able president here and now, i. e. under Kennedy himself, the USA will once again be in the position of having not only Latin America, but also Africa and Asia, i. e. the entire free world, look up to it. This seems to be the analogy Kennedy is aiming at.

Directly following this indirect propaganda for himself, Kennedy concludes his opening statement. By reintroducing the key phrase *the question is* and qualifying it so that it applies only to the immediate situation, i. e. *now*, Kennedy signals that summary remarks are to follow. Note the recurrent use of contour type [3] modified by an anticipated high pitch to cue the closure by return. Note also the shift in nuclear stress to *now*.

Ex. 40 [3] [*The question* [*now is*]] (143)
a

In closing, Kennedy restates the main points of his opening statement. In this connection, it should be mentioned that one point has already been restated once before in lines 128–129, i. e. *And I think it depends in great measure on what we do here in this country.* Its function was to ensure that the section on governmental vs. individual responsibility formed a coherent whole with the preceding sections of the text. This restatement in lines 128–129 is the first repetition of the sentential chain in lines 10–11. To be noted here is the shift in nuclear stress to include the lexical item *here*. Apart from this, the nuclear pitch configuration parallels that in example 5 above. To cue the restated lexical items *we do* and *here*, i. e. to indicate that this restatement functions as a closure by return, Kennedy modifies the nuclear pitch patterns. He uses contour type [3] instead of the neutral contour type [1].

Ex. 41 [3] [*And I think it depends* | *in great*
a

measure | *on what* [*we do* | *here*]
a

in this country] (128-129)
a

In lines 146-147 this sentential chain is taken up in a slightly modified form - Kennedy adds *in the final analysis.* In doing so he underlines that it functions as the closing closure by return in his opening statement. In this example Kennedy does not echo the nuclear pitch configuration of example 5. The topical intonational cues are used to signal the closure by return.

Ex. 42 [3] [*And I think in the final analysis* | *it*
a

depends, upon what [*we do here*]] (146-147)
a

In the closing line of his opening statement, Kennedy appeals to his fellow Americans a last time to unite in concerted action for the purpose of ensuring freedom in the world, i. e. *I think it's time America started moving again.* I would interpret this appeal as a counterproposition to the 'hypothetical' proposition *Let's stand still.* I use the term *hypothetical* proposition, because neither Kennedy nor Nixon have, in fact, proposed that the United States should stand still. However, Kennedy has been trying to prove that this is the way Nixon and the Republican Party have been acting by citing examples of where the USA hasn't made sufficient progress, implying that this is most likely what they are proposing. The intonation pattern Kennedy uses on *I think it's time America started moving again* is topical for that of a counterproposition (cf. ch. 2., exs. 31 and 32). The concave fall on *moving again* modified by extra-length signals the implicit antithesis to *standing still.* Compare line 84 for the first occurrence of *stand still.*

Ex. 43 [3] [*I think it's time* | *America started*
a

[*moving again*]] (148)
:

3. RICHARD M. NIXON'S OPENING STATEMENT

Richard M. Nixon uses a somewhat different strategy in his opening statement than Kennedy. This can be accounted for by two factors:

1) Being second in turn to speak, Nixon is forced to take a stand on what Kennedy has said in his opening statement.

2) As the Republican candidate, i. e. as candidate for the party in office, Nixon has a twofold job. Not only must he present himself and his party as the better choice in view of the course of action being proposed, but also in the light of the record of the present Administration.

These two factors determine the form his opening statement takes. The opening line itself serves as evidence for our first assertion. Commenting on Kennedy's opening statement is Nixon's foremost concern, introducing his own topic is of secondary importance for the time being.

Nixon establishes focus on Kennedy's opening statement by using the anaphoric reference item *things* coupled with the appropriate intonational cue.

Ex. 1 [*The things that Senator Kennedy* | *has*
a

[*said*] ...] (1)

The syntactic position of *things* is unusual, prepositional objects tend to occur after the preposition, for example:

Many of us can *agree with* the *things* that ...

agree with	*things*
prep. verb	prep. obj.

I think Nixon foregrounds[100] this item in order to underline the simultaneous cataphoric function it performs: the specific things Nixon is referring to in *the things* are specified in what follows. Correspondingly, the opening line of

[100]The concave fall on *things* in example 1 above not only serves as a cue for focus, but also as an intonational cue for foregrounding. See n. 98 in this connection.

Nixon's opening statement serves as the general statement in the discourse pattern general statement : examples. More important still is the use of the foregrounding technique in this instance to distract the audience's attention from the agreement mentioned at the end, i. e. its use as a rhetorical device for playing down Nixon's concession, for *backgrounding* the concession. Nixon, of course, is not keen on making even a minor concession to his opponent. The overt plot cue for backgrounding (the syntactic position of *agree with*) is complemented by the following intonational cues: postcontour position with fadeaway.

Ex. 2 ...] *many of us* | *can agree with*] (1-2)

f

With the concession backgrounded and the absence of intonational cues, how does the audience know that Nixon is making a concession? *Many of us*, by virtue of its exclusive meaning, acts as a cue for concession. It signals a reservation, implying 'not all of us'. The concession, as it stands, is nonsensical. Why would Nixon underline the fact that some people in his audience agree with Kennedy, while others do not? Such a concession would be irrelevant in his attempt to present himself as the better candidate. I would reinterpret the role the quantifier *many* plays in Nixon's concession. By using the quantifying phrase *many of us* Nixon indirectly speaks for his audience by implying an inclusive *we*-relationship, i. e. 'all of us'. *Many of us* in combination with *can*, a modal auxiliary expressing the notion of theoretical possibility, simply takes the assertiveness out of his statement. This being done, I think the quantifier *many* should be considered detached from its phrasal use. Its metonymic function in the concession is to qualify *things*. This interpretation gives a meaningful concession:

> We, i. e. all of us, can agree with many of the things that Senator Kennedy has said, but not with all of the things.

This rhetorical device is categorized as *mixtura verborum* in classical rhetoric.[101]

In support of the above interpretation we cite lines 3-10 and line 17. Lines 3-10 are a specification of the points Nixon and his audience do agree with, not a specification of *many of us*. Line 17, i. e. *Where then do we*

---

[101] Cf. Heinrich Lausberg, *Elemente der literarischen Rhetorik* (München, 1971), pp. 109-110, § 334-335.

disagree, serves as the overt plot cue for the concession as stated. It focuses on the metonymic interpretation to the effect that there are points of disagreement.

Ex. 3 ...] *where then* | *do we disagree*] (17)

a f

Note the correlation of foregrounding with , backgrounding with fadeaway both in this example and in line 1 in

the things...agree with.

f

This overt plot cue in the form of a question is preparing the focus on the reservation which follows in the form of a general statement, stating which point there is disagreement about (ll. 18–21). To be noted here is how Nixon splits up his discourse into the question : answer pattern. He simulates a dialogue, in which he fictitiously addresses the question to himself. The simulation of a dialogue in a discourse has the effect of livening up the speaker's presentation of a topic. This rhetorical device is known as *subiectio.*[102] It is characteristic for Nixon's discourse style. Compare lines 73–84 and 102–107 and the section on backgrounding in the appendix. Note that the question is reduced to a postcontour position in all of the examples.

Before we go into any more detail on Nixon's denial and refutation of Kennedy's assertions, we shall retrace our steps and point out important details omitted in our preliminary discussion of these opening lines. Thus far we have analyzed the first line of Nixon's opening statement in some detail. In this connection, we have only touched upon lines 3–10, pointing out the supportive role they play to line 1, i. e. as examples in the discourse pattern general statement : examples. In lines 3–6 and 7–10 Nixon specifies *things* by restating Kennedy's assertions. The restatements in both instances are preceded by the truth assertion *there is no question but that*, which is identical in meaning to the sentence adverbial *of course/admittedly*. "Sentence adverbials often convey the speaker's comment on the content of what he is saying."[103] In lines 3 and 7 Nixon is commenting on the indisputability of what Kennedy has said, i. e. he is presenting Kennedy's particular assertions

---

[102]Cf. Lausberg, *Handbuch*, pp. 381-382, § 771-775.

[103]Leech and Svartvik, *op. cit.*, p. 201, § 479.

as generally known 'truths'. As a result, his concession loses the appearance of being granted grudgingly – the specific things cited as examples of points Nixon is conceding require no particular discussion in view of their universal validity. Interesting to note is the intonation pattern on Nixon's truth assertion. The extra-low convex fall on *question* gives this assertion an air of finality, ruling out contradiction. Note the use of contour type [3] for the restated comment in example 5.

Ex. 4 [*There is no* [*question*]] (3)

Ex. 5 [3] [*There is no* [*question*]] (7)
a

One point should be mentioned about the latter of these two examples in the discourse pattern general statement : examples. In the second example Nixon underpins the validity of Kennedy's assertion by adding a *because*-clause explaining why it's impossible for the USA to stand still (l. 8). In this *because*-clause the lexical item *competition* is introduced into the lexical chain *struggle* (cf. l. 16 Kennedy's text). By adding the epithet *deadly* to *competition* and coupling it with an extra-high pitch and a complex nucleus, Nixon intensifies Kennedy's claim that the United States *cannot stand still.*

Ex. 6 [*because* | *we are in a* [*deadly competition*]] (8)
: 1

The anadiplotic repetition of *competition* (l. 9), signalled by a concave rise modified by an anticipated high pitch, has an emphatic effect, making Nixon's reference to the Soviet and Chinese communists as the adversaries in this *deadly competition* sound like a new point being introduced into the discussion rather than simply a restatement of what Kennedy has already said (cf. Kennedy's text ll. 14-24). The lower voice volume accompanying this section simultaneously has the effect of reducing this reference to the Soviet and Chinese communists to a mere illustrative detail to *deadly competition*. To be noted is Nixon's metonymic use of the proper nouns *Kremlin* and *Peking* to denote the Soviet and Chinese communists, and the anticipated high pitch on the first syllable of *Peking*. Lexically, *Peking* is a LEVEL STRESS word, having a prestress on its first constituent:

Pêkińg - Pe [*king*].[104]

The intonation pattern Nixon uses anticipates the Chinese communists as the other adversaries to be named (they being the only other threatening communist superpower) and, as such, meets the expectations of the audience.

Ex. 7 [2] [*a competition not only with the men in the*
a

Kremlin but the men in Pe-[*king*]] (9-10)
: a

The second repetition of *competition* in a context of grammatical cohesion (l. 11, i. e. *this competition*) serves as a link between Nixon's concession in lines 7–8 (i. e. *this nation cannot stand still*) and the proposition he now introduces in support of the present Administration and his party (i. e. *we're ahead in this competition*).

Nixon presents this proposition as an indisputable fact. He does so in an ingenious way. He asserts that Kennedy has implied that the US is ahead, witness *as Senator Kennedy I think has implied*, and then concedes that this is indeed the truth, i. e. *we're ahead in this competition ... but*. At the same time he qualifies his assertion, i. e. *as Senator Kennedy I* ***think*** *has implied*. On the surface this qualification looks like Nixon is conceding that he may be misinterpreting what Kennedy has actually said. After all, an implication of this kind is tantamount to admitting that the Eisenhower Administration (i. e. the present Administration) has done an excellent job – at least from Nixon's point of view. In reality, however, Nixon is suggesting that it is not imperative that Kennedy admits that the USA is ahead. This, in my opinion, is the underlying function of the qualification. It underlines that the proposition *we're ahead in this competition* is an indisputable fact. The foregrounding of the proposition (i. e. the foregrounding of *ahead* coupled with an anticipated high pitch) and the backgrounding of the qualified assertion lend support to this interpretation. Note the use of the concave fall to signal both the foregrounding and the concession.

Ex. 8 [2] [*We're a-* [*head in this competition*]
a :

[104]Cf. Pilch, *Manual*, ch. 2.132.

as Senator Kennedy I think has implied] (11-12)
a f

Why does Nixon actually choose this roundabout way of presenting his proposition (i. e. of suggesting that Kennedy has implied that the USA is ahead and then conceding that this is true)? By suggesting that Kennedy has admitted that the USA is ahead Nixon scores a point in his own favor. After all, it is his party, namely the Republican Party, which is responsible for this situation. By presenting his proposition as a concession Nixon scores a further point. In the reservation to his concession, i. e. *but when you're in a race the only way to stay ahead is to move ahead*, Nixon takes up Kennedy's appeal to *move ahead* and presents it as his own proposition. The concession as a whole suggests that although Kennedy is aware of the fact that the US is ahead, he has obviously overlooked another very important fact – the fact that the USA must continue making an effort if it wants to stay ahead.[105] This is a truism, or to use Lausberg's rhetorical term a *sententia*.[106] Overlooking something so self-evident does not exactly speak in favor of Kennedy. This, I think, is the implication behind Nixon's reservation. The intonation lends support to this interpretation. The extra-high concave fall on *but* and the foregrounding of *race* coupled with an anticipated high pitch focus our attention on what is to follow, leading us to expect some momentous conclusion. The truism which follows, i. e. *but when you're in a race the only way to stay ahead is to move ahead*, thwarts our expectations. The subsequent backgrounding of the truism reconciles us. It underlines the superfluity of restating such a generally known truth. What Nixon is implying, of course, is that Kennedy seems to be the only one who is unaware of this generally known 'truth'.

Ex. 9 [*but, when you're in a* [*race*] *the only way* |
1 a

---

[105]What Nixon is suggesting here stands in contradiction not only to what Kennedy has actually been proposing the whole time in his opening statement, but also to lines 7-8 in Nixon's opening statement, where he agrees with Kennedy that *this nation cannot stand still*, and to lines 14-16, where Nixon concedes that Kennedy and he agree that *the United States should move ahead*. Such is rhetoric!

[106]Cf. Lausberg, *Elemente*, pp. 38-39 and pp. 130-131, § 83 and § 398.

to stay ahead, is to move ahead] (12-13)

a

Above we said that Nixon takes up Kennedy's appeal to *move ahead* and presents it as his own proposition. This becomes evident when we expand Nixon's enthymeme into the following syllogism:

Major Premise:	When you're in a race the only way to stay ahead is to move ahead.
Minor Premise:	We're in a race and want to stay ahead.
Conclusion:	Therefore, we must move ahead.

We see that the conclusion of Nixon's argument is identical to that of Kennedy's, i. e. *this nation cannot stand still* (cf. ch. 2., p. 41). The implication of Nixon's line of argumentation, however, is: Let's keep the present Administration in office for the excellent job they've been doing and will continue to do in keeping the US in the lead. Kennedy's line of argumentation is not compatible with this. He, in reality, has been arguing that the US must *move ahead,* i. e. *do more* than it's done up to the present time, in order to prevent the Soviet Union from overtaking the US in the near future. The implication of Kennedy's line of argumentation is: The US needs better men in office to ensure that America stays in the lead. This is precisely the point that Nixon must refute in the course of his opening statement.

The other point Nixon must elaborate on is how exactly the present Administration is planning to move ahead. This is implied in Nixon's closing concession in lines 14-16, where he grants that he and Kennedy agree that *the United States should move ahead,* i. e. *And I subscribe completely to the spirit that ...* The implication is that there is disagreement on other points, i. e. what Kennedy has insinuated or actually said about the Eisenhower Administration (cf. ll. 18-21).

This closing concession could also be interpreted as implying that Kennedy and Nixon are not in agreement on *how* to move ahead, i. e. Kennedy and Nixon are in agreement on the *goals for America,* but not on *the means to reach those goals* (cf. the analogous concessions in ll. 115-117 and 162-164). Both this interpretation and the one above are equally plausible, in my opinion.

Ex. 10 [3] [*And I subscribe* | *completely, to the*

: 1 a

[spirit] that Senator Kennedy, has

expressed tonight] (14-15)

Note the concave fall on *spirit* in example 10 to cue the concession. The anticipated high pitch coupled with contour type [3] signals that this concession functions as a closure by return, as a *peroratio*[107] for lines 1-16 in Nixon's opening statement. Lines 15-16, i. e. *the spirit that the United States should move ahead*, is a specification of *spirit*. The anadiplotic repetition of *spirit*, the nuclear stress on *should* and contour type [2] simultaneously cue that this specification functions as a mere restatement of what is already expressed in the lexical item *spirit*.

Ex. 11 [2] [*the spirit that the United States*
a

[*should move ahead*]] (15-16)

Example 10 and 11 above mark the end of the first section of Nixon's opening statement. Viewed as a whole lines 1-16 function as an initial concession to Kennedy's position. Lines 17-29 in turn act as the reservation within this concession.

The reservation, a denial and refutation of Kennedy's assertion that the US *has been standing still*, can be assigned to the discourse pattern general statement : examples. The denial (ll. 18-21) takes the form of a general statement - Nixon disagrees in general that the *United States has been standing still*, he does not confine his disagreement to any specific instance Kennedy has cited as evidence for the fact that the *United States has been standing still*. In this general statement Nixon places an intonation nucleus on the actual restatement of Kennedy's assertion.

Ex. 12 [2] [*has been standing still*] (21)

[107] Cf. Lausberg, *Elemente*, p. 26 and p. 96, § 43,3 and § 296,2.

I would contend that the nuclear stress on the operator *has* does not function solely as a cue of restatement, but also singles out the proposition which is up for refutation. *Has* is followed by a second stressed element in the nucleus: the concave fall on *has* clusters with a convex fall on *still* forming a *complex nucleus.* In terms of stress the first constituent of a complex nucleus (i. e. the first cluster member) is said to carry primary stress, the second constituent (i. e. the second cluster member) is said to carry a tertiary stress. In terms of pitch the complex nucleus could be described as follows: the second pitch pattern of a complex nucleus "covers a much narrower interval than the first, starting lower in the case of falling pitch, higher in the case of rising pitch."[108]

Placed on the assertion which is being refuted, the complex nucleus has both an emphatic and antithetical function. The point Nixon is stressing is that the United States ***was not*** and ***is not*** *standing still* under the present Administration. The present perfect progressive tense expresses this complex time relation between past and present. From the overall context in which it is being used, it should be apparent what exact time span the present perfect progressive is referring to (i. e. the period of office of the present Administration - the last 7 1/2 years (ll. 44-45)). By using *has* rather than some other preverbal modifier, Nixon indicates to his audience that it is this time span (or a time span within this time span) that he is focusing on. This time reference (*past-time-related-to-present-time*)[109] is essential for Nixon's defense of the present Administration, it is essential if Nixon is to prove that the USA has made progress under the present Administration.

The actual refutation of Kennedy's assertion, i. e. the examples Nixon gives to back his general statement, supports the above interpretation. In his refutation Nixon focuses on the two preceding years of the Administration's period of office (1958-1959), singling out the growth of GNP to prove that the USA *has not been standing still.* He begins by restating Kennedy's assertion that the growth of GNP in the USA in 1958 *was the lowest of any industrial nation in the world* (ll. 22-24; cf. ll. 51-53 in Kennedy's opening statement). To distract our attention from this fact Nixon foregrounds *last year,* forcing Kennedy's restated comment into the background. Contour type [3] signals the restatement.

---

[108]Pilch, *Ms. 1,* p. 129 and pp. 155-160.

[109]Leech and Svartvik, *op. cit.,* p. 65, § 112. For a detailed discussion of the possibilities of the present perfect compare Alfred Schopf, *Das Verzeitungssystem des Englischen und seine Textfunktion* (Tübingen, 1984), pp. 320-331.

Ex. 13 [3] [... *that our, growth in national product,*

last [*year*] *was the lowest of any*

industrial nation in the world] (23-24)

f

Taking it for granted that his audience is familiar with the business cycle, Nixon goes on to restate the fact that *last year* was the year 1958, i. e. *now last year of course was 1958.* What he is implying, of course, is that Kennedy's assertion is true but insignificant - *1958*, as everybody knows, was *a recession year* and recession years always go hand in hand with a minimal growth in GNP. The echoing postcontour on the specification which follows, i. e. *that happened to be a recession year,* lends support to this interpretation. It signals that this specification is a mere restatement of the preceding statement.

Ex. 14 [2] [*Now last year of course* | *was nineteen*

: a

fifty [*eight*] *that happened to be* |

a recession year] (24-26)

a

To actually demonstrate that the US *has* **not** *been standing still,* Nixon now compares the growth of GNP in 1958 and 1959, quoting statistical figures as proof of the nation's progress (ll. 25-29). The comparison is in the form of an antithesis. To cue the antithesis Nixon uses the topical intonational cues.

Ex.15a [3] [... *that our, growth in national product,*

last [*year*] ...] (23)

Ex.15b [*but when we look* | *at the growth of GNP,*

[*this year*] ...] (26-27)
1

Ex.16a ...] *that happened to be* | *a recession year*] (25-26)
a

Ex.16b ...] *a year of recovery*][110] (27)

Ex.17a ...] *was the lowest of any industrial* ...] (23-24)

Ex.17b [... *and one of the* [*highest*] *in the*
1

world today] (28-29)

Having completed his refutation, Nixon uses the digressional phrase *more about that later* to simultaneously mark the completion of reservations voiced with respect to his concession in lines 1-16. The use of the postcontour and the fast speech tempo coupled with a fadeaway serves as an unmistakable intonational cue that Nixon is about to change his topic.

Ex. 18 ...] *more about that later*] (29)
f

Nixon introduces focus on his new topic by using the topical intonational cue. In addition, he places a precontour stress on the grammatical word *to* (a cue for restatement) to indicate that he is going to focus on a topic which has already been broached.

Ex. 19 [*Looking then* | *to this problem* | *of* ...] (30)

The topic Nixon focuses on is *how the United States should move ahead and where the United States is moving* (ll. 30-32). Kennedy has dealt with *this problem of where the United States is moving* in his opening statement, i. e.

[110]Note the use of the echoing postcontour to signal that a *year of recovery* functions as a restatement of *this year*, parallel to example 14 above.

his enumeration of instances of where the US has not done a satisfactory job (ll. 49–94), proposing individual initiative backed by effective governmental action (ll. 97–122) as the answer to the problem of *how the United States should move ahead.* In denying that the United States has been standing still, Nixon has also briefly touched upon the question of *where the United States is moving* (see above).

Ex. 20 [3] [...*of how the United States,*
1

[*should* | *move ahead*]] (30-31)

Ex. 21 [3] [*and where the United States*
1

[*is moving*]] (31-32)

Note the distribution of nuclear and precontour pitch patterns to cue the antithesis. The nuclear stress on the auxiliaries *should* and *is* coupled with contour type [3] serves as a cue of restatement.

This focus reflects what Nixon's opening statement, in essence, is about. Therefore, I would interpret lines 30–32 as the topic sentence of Nixon's opening statement. All remaining sections deal with this topic: Nixon gives an account of the accomplishments of the present Administration (a more detailed discussion of the topic *where the United States is moving*; ll. 50–84) and proposes a course of action for the future (discussion of the topic *how the United States should move ahead*; ll. 86–153).

Nixon approaches the problem of *where the United States is moving* by suggesting to his audience that they join him in *looking at the record.* To underline the universal validity of his approach, Nixon uses the *auctoritas* device[111], appealing to an (at this stage) unnamed authority, i. e. a *very famous campaigner*[112] (ll. 32–33). What Nixon is suggesting, of course, is that

---

[111] Cf. Lausberg, *Elemente*, p. 45, § 106, and Lausberg, *Handbuch*, pp. 234-235, § 426.

[112] The *very famous campaigner* Nixon is citing is Alfred Emanuel Smith, who showed "extraordinary ability as a vote-getter" (*Encyclopaedia Britannica*, 1953 ed., p. 827). He was governor of New York State for four terms (1918-1920 and 1922-1928) - the first man in the history of New York

the record of the Eisenhower Administration, like that of the *very famous campaigner*, is exemplary.

Before actually consulting the record of the Eisenhower Administration to support his position, Nixon again denies that the United States *has been standing still* (l. 35; cf. above in this connection). This second denial is in the form of a focalizing question and focuses on the ***is** not standing still* implied in *has not been standing still*. Note the nuclear stress on *is* cuing the restatement, while the complex nucleus re-emphasizes that this is the proposition which is up for refutation.

Ex. 22 [*Is the United States standing still*] (35)
1

This second denial in the form of a focalizing question is followed by two restatements, also focalizing questions. An introductory *it*-construction (i. e. *Is it true*) precedes the actual restatements, emphasizing that what is to follow is, of course, not true. The extra-low convex fall on *true* gives the introductory *it*-construction an air of finality. (Cf. ch. 3, ex. 4 and 5). Note the use of contour type [3] for the restated *it*-construction.

Ex. 23 [*Is it* [*true*,]...] (36)

Ex. 24 [3] [*Is it* [*true*,]...] (39)
a

The first restatement (ll. 36–38) is a summary enumeration of the negative attributes Kennedy has ascribed to the present Administration. By emphasizing each negative attribute in this enumeration, Nixon is in fact making it stand out as one up for refutation. The pitch configuration on these items is topical for the discourse pattern enumeration. The extra-length modifi-

State to have this honour. In 1928 he was the Democratic candidate for the presidency, but was defeated by the Republican candidate Herbert Hoover. In his campaign speeches he is quoted to have said: "*Let's look at the record.*" Cf. John Bartlett, *Familiar Quotations*, ed. Christopher Morley and Louella D. Everett 12th ed. (London, 1949), p. 842. Nixon, presumably, does not name Smith as the *very famous campaigner*, because he takes it for granted that his audience knows who he is referring to.

cation on the pitch patterns in the precontour and the pauses[113] between the enumerated items produce the emphatic effect referred to above.

Ex. 25 [2] [*has been an Administration of retreat,*

a :

of defeat, of stag- [*nation*]] (37-38)

: a

In his second restatement (ll. 39–42), Nixon makes reference to a specific field Kennedy has mentioned in his opening statement where the USA has supposedly been standing still, i. e. *the field of electric power.* His renewed use of the focalizing question to stress the contrary of what Kennedy has originally asserted adds emotional color to his denials. The backgrounding of *have not been moving ahead* suggests that further focalizing questions are superfluous – by now it should be more than evident that the US *has* ***not*** *been standing still.* It is high time that Nixon adduced evidence to refute what Kennedy has asserted. Note the clustering of the concave fall on a preverbal modifier[114] (this time on *not*) with the convex fall on *ahead* (echoing the complex nucleus of exs. 12 and 22) to single out this statement for refutation.

Ex. 26 ...] *we have not been moving ahead*] (41-42)

f

To prove that his own assertions are not unfounded, Nixon consults the record of the Eisenhower Administration. His tactic is not to merely cite examples from this record, but rather to compare it to that of the previous Administration – the Truman Administration.[115] This plan is stated in lines 43-46.

---

[113]Cf. Henning Wode, "Englische Satzintonation," *Phonetica* 15 (1966), 199-201.

[114]This analysis of *not* as a preverbal modifier is based on Jan W. F. Mulder and Sándor G. J. Hervey, *The Strategy of Linguistics* (Edinburgh, 1980), pp. 157 ff.

[115]For the reader who is unfamiliar with American politics, it should be added that Truman and Kennedy had the same party affiliation – they were both Democrats. Therefore, it is only natural that Nixon should choose

After emphatically restating[116] his own assertion,

Ex. 27 [3] [*I think we find that America* [*has been*
a : a

moving ahead]] (48-49)

Nixon employs the plot cue *let us take* to signal the beginning of his list of binary antithetical examples. This plot cue is employed three times (ll. 50, 54 and 58). It occurs solely in the precontour, the focus of *take* receives the nuclear stress. In the first two instances (ll. 50 and 54) *let us* appears in its contracted form *let's*. The intonation contour in both these instances is identical: contour type [2] with a concave fall in the precontour on *let's* and a convex fall in the nucleus on the respective foci *schools* and *power*.

Ex. 28 [2] [*Let's take* [*schools*]] (50)

Ex. 29 [2] [*Let's take hydroelectric* [*power*]] (54)

The third time Nixon uses this plot cue *let's* appears in its uncontracted form *let us*. As in the preceding instances *let us* receives a precontour stress: a concave fall spans the whole of the uncontracted form. In contrast to the

the Truman Administration as the basis for his comparison. The Administration which preceded the Truman Administration, i. e. the Roosevelt Administration (1933-1945), was, it is true, also Democratic. It was presumably too far in the past to serve as the basis for a sensible comparison. One could, of course, also speculate that the record of the Roosevelt Administration was 'too good' to serve as the basis for a comparison which must turn out in favor of the Eisenhower Administration. In his opening statement, Kennedy has depicted Franklin Roosevelt as an exemplary president, but not even mentioned Harry Truman. Cf. p. 55 in this connection.

116 This restatement serves as the closure-by-return conclusion to the first section of the discourse pattern general statement : examples, i. e. it winds up the general-statement section before the speaker turns to the example section.

preceding instances, however, Nixon uses contour type [1] and places a *low* convex fall on the focus *hospitals*. In addition, he modifies the convex fall by an extra-high pitch.

Ex. 30 [*Let us* | *take* [*hospitals*]] (58)
1

A low convex fall topically signals finality. When modified by an extra-high pitch it has a climactic effect. In view of this I would be inclined to interpret examples 28, 29 and 30 as a climactic series and not merely as a succession of cues used solely for the purpose of signalling the antithetical examples which follow. Examples 28 und 29 constitute the non-final constituents in this series. In support of this interpretation we quote Pilch, who claims that contour type [2] topically signals an absence of focus and cites the non-final constituents of climactic series as a particular case of such an absence of focus.[117]

The intonation of the respective antithetical examples serves as additional support for the above interpretation. It runs contrary to the intonation of the plot cues. This creates a certain suspense, and ultimately reinforces the *climax* on *let us take hospitals*. Let's delve a bit deeper into this point. In contrast to the non-climactic intonation on *let's take schools/hydroelectric power* both the antithetical example in lines 50–53 and in lines 54–57 are characterized by an internal climax. The sequence of concave rises (a rising pitch frequently anticipates a climax) culminating in an extra-low convex fall signals this internal climax. To be noted in example 31 (see below) is Nixon's simultaneous use of an overt plot cue to signal the internal climax, i. e. *for that matter*. Note also the use of contour type [3] to cue the restated words *schools* and *power*.

Ex. 31 [3] [*We have built more* [*schools*] *in these*
1 a

last | *seven and a half years*] (50-51)
a

[*than we built in the previous seven and a*
a

[117] Cf. Pilch, *Manual*, ch. 6.324.

half | *for that matter* | *in the previous*
a

[*twenty years*]] (50-53)

Ex. 32 [3] [*We have developed, more hydroelectric*
1 a

[*power*] *in these seven and a half years*]
a

[*than was developed in* [*any previous*

Administration in history]] (54-57)

The respective antithetical example to *let us take hospitals* is not climactic. On the contrary, there is an absence of focus on this example cued by contour type [2].

Ex. 33 [2] [*We find that more have been built, in this*
a :

Administration | *than in the* [*previous*

Administration]] (58-60)

The climactic intonation in examples 31 and 32 leads us to expect a 'genuine' climax in example 33. The non-climactic intonation in example 33 indicates that ***the climax*** is already contained within the plot cue to this example, i. e. the climactic *let us take hospitals* (cf. above). Example 33 merely functions as a confirmation of this climax by underlining that further comparisons are not necessary - the result will merely be the same, everyone is already convinced that the record of the Eisenhower Administration is better than that of the Truman Administration. This is reconfirmed by the fast speech tempo and the fadeaway on *highways* in the subsequent fourth example.

Ex. 34 [2] [*The same is true of* [*highways*]] (60)

f

Instead of summarizing and switching the topic at this point, however, Nixon introduces the plot cue for restatement *let's put it in terms...* to indicate that he is not yet finished with his comparison of the Truman and Eisenhower Administration. He restates his claim by comparing the growth in GNP in both Administrations. In choosing this topic Nixon a) creates a link between this section and the previous section where he has dealt with this topic (ll. 22-30), and b) broaches a topic which interests all Americans. Nixon is taking it for granted that everyone knows that growth in GNP reflects the prosperity of the nation as a whole - something which directly affects each and every American.

In lines 71-72 Nixon narrows down the circle of *all of us* to include only the average family and once more restates his claim, proving that there was an increase in the average family income in the Eisenhower Administration.

For important intonational characteristics in lines 61-85 see the appendix pages 106 and 110.

To indicate that he has completed his list of binary antithetical examples, Nixon uses a twofold plot cue: *Now* and *this is not standing still. Now* has a deictic function[118], it signals that Nixon is re-focusing on the fact that the USA *is not standing still*, i. e. that Nixon is closing by returning to his assertion in lines 48-49.

Ex. 35 [3] [*Now*] (85)

Ex. 36 [3] [*This is not standing* [*still*]] (85)

a

This closure by return

1) marks the completion of Nixon's first main topic, i. e. *where the United States is moving*. In the form of an equational syntagm with *standing still* as the predicate noun, it has the effect of reinforcing Nixon's refutation, suggesting that whatever else one may say about the examples given

[118] This interpretation corresponds to Halliday and Hasan's analysis of *now*. Cf. Halliday and Hasan, *op. cit.*, p. 264.

above to refute Kennedy's assertion (i. e. *this*) one thing is definitely false - that they show even the faintest trace of standing still.

2) anticipates that Nixon is about to start on his second main topic, i. e. *how the United States should move ahead.*

Nixon creates a link between these two topics by taking up the lexical chain *record* and indicates his shift in focus by using a concession as transitional device. The concession is partial, only the reservation is given. The point that Nixon is conceding (i. e. *it's a good record*) is merely implied in the restatement following the plot cue for concession *but*, i. e. *good as this record is.*

Ex. 37 [2] [*But*, *good as this record* [*is*] *may I*
1 a a

emphasize, it isn't enough] (86-87)
a

The concave fall on *but* has a twofold function: it establishes focus and cues the concession. The nuclear stress on *is* coupled with contour type [2] cues the restatement. Of further interest is the foregrounded lexical item *good*, which is operative in determining the form the reservation takes: an antithetical *not enough* (or a semantically equivalent phrase) is called for to complete the reservation. The anticipated high pitch on the proclitic syllable of *enough* bears this out. Note the convex fall plus the concave fall and vice versa to signal the antithesis *is ... good* vs. *isn't ... enough.*

Nixon follows up the reservation with a restatement in the form of a general proposition, the latter in turn in the form of a sentential antithesis: *A record is never something to stand on, it's something to build on* (ll. 87-88; cf. n. 106). To cue the restatement Nixon uses contour type [2]. Noteworthy is his use of the *reverse echo* to signal the antithetical specification *a record is something to build on.*

Ex. 38 [2] [*A record is* [*never something to stand on*]
1

it's something to build on] (87-88)

This proposition, or to be more precise *building on the record of the Eisenhower Administration*, is Nixon's general answer to the question of *how the United States should move ahead.* The chain link in the following line, i. e. *and in building on this record* (ll. 88-89), proves that this is *how* Nixon and his party plan to *move ahead.*

This chain link is followed by the particular assertion *I believe that we have the secret for progress.* The nuclear stress on *we* indicates that the referent of *we* has switched to Nixon and the Republican Party. In addition, it is to be understood as a cue of antithesis, i. e. *we* in contrast to Kennedy and the Democratic Party (cf. ch. 2., n. 68 and ch. 2., ex. 4 in this connection).

Ex. 39 [4] [*And in building on this record* | *I believe* | *that,* [*we have the secret*] *for progress*] (88-89)

Contour type [4] indicates that Nixon is presenting his particular assertion as an apodictic statement (cf. ch. 2., ex. 15 and 39 in this connection). Nevertheless, he substantiates his claim by giving the following reasons for his conviction:[119]

1) the record of the Eisenhower Administration proves that *we*, i. e. Nixon and his party, *know the way* (ll. 90-91).

2) Kennedy has only the old Truman record and programs to offer, which are inferior (as *I*, i. e. Nixon, have already proved).

3) *We* (Nixon and his party) are in favor of programs which stand for progress, or so *we believe. Our belief* in our programs is not unfounded in

[119] *First of all* functions as a plot cue for the first reason. At the same time, it indicates that Nixon is going to give at least one more reason in support of his assertion. The further reasons are not signalled by plot cues, but we have to interpret them as such from the overall context (ll. 92-124).

view of our record, i. e. the record of the Eisenhower Administration, in whose footsteps we are following.

Let us look at the second reason in a bit more detail. In lines 92-93 Nixon asserts that Kennedy is convinced that he himself *knows the way*. Nixon concedes that Kennedy no doubt means well (i. e. *I respect the sincerity with which he makes that suggestion*), but the truth of the matter is that Kennedy *cannot* know the way to progress - he isn't even offering new programs, but is wedded to the old, inferior ones. His are as Nixon metaphorically characterizes Kennedy's programs *simply retreads of the programs of the Truman Administration*.

In lines 98-100 Nixon seeks to corroborate this claim by challenging Kennedy to prove him wrong, implying, of course, that Kennedy *cannot*. His programs are undoubtedly the *old* ones. Consequently, there is nothing more to be said on the topic of Kennedy's programs. The intonation pattern on *are new* - the intonational cue for closure by return - bears this out.

Ex. 40 [3] [*in which, his programs* | *are*
a

[*new*]] (100)

Nixon follows up this closure by return with a restatement (ll. 100-101). In this restatement he takes up the lexical chain *progress* from line 89 and combines it with *more* to serve as the basis for a characterization of his own versus Kennedy's programs. By placing the nuclear stress on *more progress* Nixon underlines his belief that Kennedy's programs will not prove to be better than Truman's. The nuclear stress on *more*[120] has an antithetical effect, emphasizing that Kennedy's programs will *not* mean more progress *than we had then*. In order to mean *more* progress than *we* had then they would have to be better than those of the Eisenhower Administration. Since they're only *retreads* of Truman's programs though, they can by no means be better than those of the Eisenhower Administration. As a result, Kennedy's programs can impossibly mean *more* progress for the USA than his own programs, which

[120]As a rule *more* is not given nuclear stress. Cf. Esser, *op. cit.*, p. 57 and p. 89. Cf. also in this connection ch. 2., ex. 26b. Our empirical observations, however, show that the nucleus is frequently shifted forward to *more* to mark an implicit antithesis.

are at least on a par with those of the Eisenhower Administration, if not better. Note contour type [2] to cue the restatement and the *reverse echo* to cue the implicit antithesis between *than we had then* and what we are going to have under a Kennedy Administration.

Ex. 41 [2] [*where they will mean* | [*more progress*]

than we had then...] (100-101)

Having already, by contrast, implied that his own party's programs *do* mean progress, Nixon's next step is to present these programs. To introduce this topic Nixon uses the rhetorical device *subiectio* again (cf. n. 102). Note the backgrounding of the question as in example 3 in this chapter.

Ex. 42 ...] *what kind of programs* | *are we for*] (102)
1 f

To cue his answer[121] Nixon repeats the lexical chain introduced in his question (i. e. *we are for programs*), placing a concave rise on the last item of this repetition (i. e. on *programs*). Note the extra-high concave fall on *we* to cue the implicit antithesis *we* (the Republican Party) ≠ *they* (the Democratic Party). Compare the extra-high concave fall on *we for* in example 42 above, which seems to fulfill the same function.

Ex. 43 [*We are for programs* | ... (103)
1 :

Nixon presents his answer in lines 103-110. His presentation is weak, it consists solely in the praise of his programs. Nixon does not truly specify the *kind of programs* he and his party advocate, but merely gives a checklist of items making his programs desirable. He merely stresses the positive direction in which his programs are tending.

In lines 103-104 Nixon emphasizes that his party is for programs which *will expand educational opportunities*. What Nixon is implying, of course, is that his party is against programs that will cut back on educational oppor-

[121] In line 18 Nixon uses the same technique to cue his answer.

tunities - but then, who isn't? Note the concave fall modified by extra-length to cue the implicit antithesis *expand* vs. *cut back on*.

Ex. 44 [*We are for programs* | *that will ex-* [*pand*
1 : :

educational opportunities] (103-104)

Before turning to the second item on his checklist, Nixon restates in more specific terms what *expanding educational opportunities* means. It means giving ***all*** *Americans their equal chance for education*; and, for that matter, giving all Americans their equal chance wherever this is not the case at present. The vagueness of this restatement underlines that Nixon is not really specifying his programs.

To signal the second item on his checklist (ll. 109-110) Nixon uses a slightly modified version of the plot cue *we are for programs* - he adds the item *in addition*. Note the shift in stress to this new item (cf. ex. 43 above).

Ex. 45 [*We are for programs* | *in addition* ... (108)
:

The second item making Nixon's programs desirable is his concern for the aged and the fact that they deserve better medical care. His fumbling about for the right words in line 109 leaves us with the impression that Nixon is unable to specify his programs and therefore resorts to empty statements of mere praise for his programs.

Nixon retains this focus of *better medical care for the aged* in lines 111-114, making it the basis for a renewed concession to the effect that Kennedy has good intentions (i. e. he also wants to help the aged - *we both want to help the old people* (ll. 112-114)), but lacks the potential to carry them out, i. e. his programs are inadequate to reach the goals he has set himself (cf. ll. 93-94 for the original concession). This restated concession is cued by the deictic phrase *here again* and the lexical item *want to*, a link in the lexical chain *sincere* (l. 93).

There is a more general concession underlying the concession as stated above:

Kennedy and Nixon are in agreement as to the goals for America, but not as to the means to reach those goals.

This concession, in turn, can be viewed as a more specific restatement of the concession in lines 14–15 (cf. ex. 10 in this chapter). As above, the restatement here is also cued by the phrase *here again*. The concession and reservation respectively are cued by the phrasal chains *agree on the goals/disagree on the means*. Nixon does not use expressly these phrasal chains. Instead, he a) modifies the first phrasal chain by using the rhetorical device *litotes*, i. e. *not in disagreement as to the aim* (l. 112) and b) uses Kennedy's key phrase *the question is*, rather than the direct chain link *disagree on*, to state the reservation, i. e. *the question is the means*. By asserting that the real question is not the goals but the means Nixon outdoes Kennedy, he uses Kennedy's rhetorical device to his own advantage. What Nixon is actually implying, of course, is that America cannot keep its leading position with the means that Kennedy is advocating. This is confirmed in the restatement in lines 115–117. Note a) the use of contour type [2] to cue the restatement and b) the use of the concave vs. the convex fall to cue the antithesis *means that I advocate* vs. *means that he advocates*.

Ex. 46 [2] [*I think that the means* | *that* [*I advocate*] :

will reach that goal | *better than the*
f

means that he advocates] (115-117)
a f

To conclude the presentation of his party's programs Nixon simply lists the other areas where these programs are supposedly better than Kennedy's (ll. 119–121). This list is preceded by a concession, i. e. *I could give better examples* (l. 118). This concession, in my opinion, can only be interpreted as an ANTICLIMAX.[122] The listener expects a *peroratio* (cf. n. 107). Instead, Nixon only suggests that he ***could give better examples***. The question, of course, is why doesn't Nixon do so, if he in fact knows some better examples. The fast speech tempo coupled with a fadeaway and contour type [2] cues the absence of focus on this concession and as such underlines the *anticlimax*.

[122] Cf. Pilch, *Manual*, ch. 6.023 (iii).

Ex. 47 [2] [*I could give* [*better examples*] *but for* f

for #] (118)

Nixon closes by returning to his original proposition, i. e. *a record is something to build on* (cf. ll. 87-88). By taking up the race image to generally characterize his programs, i. e. *we have programs which...will move America* (cf. the lexical chain *stay ahead - move ahead* in l. 13), Nixon establishes a link between his original proposition and his present sub-focus. Programs which stand for progress make it possible to build on the excellent record of the Eisenhower Administration. This closure by return (see below) completes the first sub-focus of Nixon's second main topic - *how the United States should move ahead.* Note the echoing postcontour to cue that Nixon is restating the fact that this *wonderful record* is the result of *seven and a half years* of effort.

Ex. 48 [3] [*move her forward* | *and build on the* a

[*wonderful record*] *that we have made,*

over these past seven and a half a

years] (122-124)

In line 125 Nixon introduces the second sub-focus of the topic *how the United States should move ahead.* He still focuses on the topic *programs*, but from a different angle, i. e. from the angle of costs. To establish this *re-focus*[123] he uses the plot cue *now* plus the anaphoric reference item *these programs* and continues by introducing the following proposition[124]:

[123]Note that the term *re-focus* [our coin], as used above, means focusing on the same topic but in a different way. Compare ch. 3., ex. 35, where it simply means to focus on the same topic again.

[124]This proposition can be assigned to the discourse pattern proposition : counterproposition. See below for the counterproposition.

The test of a program is how much you're spending.

or:

The more you spend, the better the program.

In suggesting that this proposition is questionable (i. e. by qualifying it - *in evaluating them we often have a tendency...* - (l. 126)), Nixon is already hinting that it, or to be more precise, the conclusion of the syllogism underlying this proposition is up for refutation. The syllogism could be stated as follows:

Major Premise:	The more you spend, the better the program.
Minor Premise:	Kennedy is spending more.
Conclusion:	Therefore, Kennedy's program is better.

Before actually refuting this proposition, Nixon concedes that the costs of Kennedy's programs are calculated higher than the costs of his own programs. In a short digression, cued by the ironic *I costed out the cost of the Democratic platform,* Nixon cites the figures which support his assertion that Kennedy's programs will entail more expenditures (ll. 131-139).

In lines 140-141 the original proposition (i. e. the conclusion of the syllogism underlying this proposition) is explicitly questioned - *Does this mean that his program is better than ours?* This question, in my opinion, is not a focalizing question. It does not follow the pattern of the focalizing questions encountered thus far in Nixon's and Kennedy's opening statements. Instead, it a) has the topical intonation for *queries*[125]: a rising pitch pattern in the nucleus (modified here by an extra-high pitch and extra-length),

Ex. 49 [*Does this mean that his program is*
a 

[better than ours]] (140-141)
 1:

and b) is directly followed by an answer, i. e. *not at all.* This answer functions as the denial in the discourse pattern denial : refutation. Note the complex nucleus cuing that a refutation is to follow.

Ex. 50 [2] [*not at all*] (142)

[125]Cf. Pilch, *Manual,* ch. 6.124.

The refutation is given as a counterproposition (ll. 142–145). This counterproposition is antithetical in form. Paraphrased, it reads as follows:

> The test of a program is not how much one spends, but what one spends on.

Nixon's implicit syllogism in support of his own programs, then, is:

Major Premise:	Spending money in the right way is the test of a better program.
Minor Premise:	We're spending money in the right way.
Conclusion:	Therefore, our program is better.

To drive his point home, i. e. that his programs are better than Kennedy's, Nixon resorts to his checklist technique of proof again (cf. ch. 3., exs. 43 f.), instead of giving the required specification of what is meant by spending money in the right way, i. e. by doing the *right things*. He introduces the item *stimulate* into the lexical chain *progress*, *move*[126] and stresses that his programs *will stimulate the creative energies of a hundred and eighty million free Americans* (ll. 146–148). Such programs are necessarily *better programs*. Nixon's qualification of his assertion, i. e. *And in our case I do believe* (ll. 145–146), does not truly function as such. The emphatic nucleus on *do*[127] and the simultaneous use of contour type [4] (see below) indicates that this assertion is to be interpreted as an apodictic statement (cf. ch. 2., ex. 15). This is further underlined by the extra-high pitch on *stimulate* (see below). Note Nixon's use of the *reverse echo* to cue the specification that it is the *creative energies of* ***a hundred and eighty million free Americans*** which must be stimulated.

Ex. 51 [4] [*And in our case, I* [*do believe*] *that*
a

our programs,] [*will stimulate the*
a 1

[126] *Stimulate*, by virtue of its semantic equivalence to *progress* and *move*, functions as a chain link between this sub-focus (ll. 125-153) and the preceding sub-focus (ll. 86-125) of *how the United States should move ahead*.

[127] Cf. Quirk *et al.*, *op. cit.*, pp. 694-695, ch. 10.57.

cre-[ative, energies] of a hundred
a

and eighty | million, free Americans] (145-148)
a

This mere accumulation of lexical items having a positive connotation, i. e. ***stimulate, creative** energies, **a hundred and eighty million free** Americans*, has the effect of emphasizing the superiority of Nixon's programs. Objectively it cannot, of course, be regarded as real evidence that Nixon's programs are better than Kennedy's.

In lines 150 and 152 Nixon extends his checklist of items to include words having a negative connotation, i. e. the antithetical *stifle* and *stagnation*[128], and asserts that Kennedy's programs *will have a tendency to stifle* (vs. *stimulate*) *those creative energies* (ll. 149-150) and *would lead to the stagnation* (vs. *animation*) *of the motive power* needed for progress (ll. 151-153). Here again, the mere accumulation of words (this time with a negative connotation) does not actually serve as evidence that Kennedy's programs are inferior, all the more so because Nixon's assertions prove to be mere suppositions. Nixon not only qualifies both of these assertions, i. e. *I believe* (l. 148 and 150), but also adds the non-committal phrases ***will have a tendency** to stifle* and ***would lead** to the stagnation* ... To be rhetorically effective, Nixon should have been sure that Kennedy's programs ***will** stifle* and ***will** lead to stagnation.*

It should be noted that the antithesis set up in lines 145-153, i. e. *stimulate ≠ stifle* and *animation ≠ stagnation*, slightly changes the gist of Nixon's line of argumentation. The antithesis expresses a clear *either/or* alternative. In doing so it suggests that it is not anymore a question of voting for the party which will mean ***more** progress* vs. ***less** progress* for the USA[129], but a question of voting for the party which will mean progress *at all.* This antithesis completes Nixon's second main topic - *how the United States should move ahead.*

---

[128]Nixon has already used this lexical item, i. e. *stagnation*, to suggest that Kennedy has ascribed this characteristic to the Eisenhower Administration. Cf. ch. 3., ex. 25. ***Stagnation*** stands in antithesis to the implicit *animation.*

[129]Nixon has already suggested that it is a matter of voting for the party which *will mean more progress* for the USA. Cf. ll. 100-101, where Nixon stresses this fact and our analysis in ch. 3., ex. 41.

To indicate that he's bringing his opening statement to a close Nixon uses the transitional device *the final point that I would like to make is this.* Unimportant in itself, this transitional device is in the postcontour and is accompanied by fadeaway and a fast speech tempo.

Ex. 52]...*the final point that I would like to make* |

is this] (154)
f

In this final section Nixon closes by returning to the key idea of his opening statement – *we agree on the goals, but not on the means.* To lead up to this closure by return Nixon takes up the *sincerity*-theme again. This is easily done by implying that Kennedy has suggested that the Republican Party lacks *compassion for the poor.* Nixon, of course, asserts this isn't so. No matter what Kennedy might believe, no one else can have any reason to doubt the *sincerity* of the Republican Party. To equalize fronts Nixon shifts focus from *we* to *I*, stressing the *sincerity* of his own motives and at the same time magnanimously ascribing the same *sincerity* to Kennedy's motives (cf. l. 93 for the original concession). After a short refutation in lines 159-160, Nixon once again stresses his and Kennedy's mutual *sincerity*, i. e. *I know Senator Kennedy feels as deeply about these problems as I do.* This concession serves as a cue for the closure by return which concludes Nixon's opening statement.

The closure by return outwardly takes the form of a reservation, signalled by the overt plot cue *but.* Closer scrutiny, however, brings to light the restated concession *agree on the goals* followed by the restated reservation *disagree on the means.* Note the concave fall on *goals for America* in example 53 below to cue the concession and contour type [3] in both examples below to cue the closure by return. The anticipated high pitch and fadeaway accompanying the reservation has an anticlimactic effect, giving the listener the impression that Nixon is only attaching secondary importance to the fact that he and Kennedy are not in agreement as to how the United States should move ahead. This is improbable. Consequently, I would interpret Nixon's *anticlimax* as unintentional, as a case of poor rhetoric – a mere reflection of the fact that he has run out of new things to say.

Ex. 53 [3] [*but our disagreement, is not about the*
a a

[*goals* | *for America*]] (162-163)

Ex. 54 [3] [*but only, about the* [*means* | *to reach*
1 a f

those goals]] (163-164)

APPENDIX

KENNEDY'S OPENING STATEMENT

(Orthographic Transcription)

In the election of 1860 Abraham Lincoln said the
question was whether this nation could exist
half slave or half free.
In the election of 1960, and with the world around us,
the question is whether the world will exist
half slave or half free,
whether it will move in the direction of freedom,
in the direction of the road that we are taking,
or whether it will move in the direction of slavery.

I think it will depend in great measure upon what
we do here in the United States,

      on the kind of society that we build,
      on the kind of strength that we maintain.

We discuss tonight domestic issues, but I would not
want that to be any implication to be given that this
does not involve directly our struggle with Mr.
Khrushchev for survival. Mr. Khrushchev is in New
York and he maintains the communist offensive throughout
the world, because of the productive power of the
Soviet Union itself.
The Chinese communists have always had a large
population, but they are important and dangerous now
because they are mounting a major effort within their
own country.

The kind of country we have here,
the kind of society we have,
the kind of strength we build in the United States
will be the defense of freedom.

If we do well here, if we meet our obligations, if
we're moving ahead, then I think freedom will be secure
around the world.
If we fail, then freedom fails.

Therefore, I think the question before the American people is:

> Are we doing as much as we can do?
> Are we as strong as we should be?
> Are we as strong as we must be,

if we're going to maintain our independence? -
And if we're going to maintain and hold out the hand of friendship to those who look to us for assistance, to those who look to us for survival?

I should make it very clear that I do not think we're doing enough, that I am not satisfied as an American with the progress that we're making.
This is a great country, but I think it could be a greater country.
And this is a powerful country, but I think it could be a more powerful country.

I'm not satisfied to have fifty per cent of our steel mill capacity unused.
I'm not satisfied when the United States had last year the lowest rate of economic growth of any major industrialized society in the world, because economic growth means strength and vitality, it means we're able to sustain our defenses, it means we're able to meet our commitments abroad.
I'm not satisfied when we have over nine billion dollars worth of food, some of it rotting, even though there is a hungry world, and even though four million Americans wait every month for a food package from the government, which averages five cents a day per individual. I saw cases in West Virginia, here in the United States, where children took home part of their school lunch in order to feed their families, because I don't think we're meeting our obligations towards these Americans.
I'm not satisfied when the Soviet Union is turning out twice as many scientists and engineers as we are.
I'm not satisfied when many of our teachers are inadequately paid or when our children go to school part

time shifts. I think we should have an educational system second to none.
I'm not satisfied when I see men like Jimmy Hoffa, in charge of the largest union in the United States, still free.
I'm not satisfied when we are failing to develop the natural resources of the United States to the fullest. Here in the United States, which developed the Tennessee Valley and which built the Grand Coulee and the other dams in the Northwest United States, at the present rate of hydropower production - and that is the hallmark of an industrialized society - the Soviet Union by 1975 will be producing more power than we are.

These are all the things I think in this country that can make our society strong or can mean that it stands still.

I'm not satisfied until every American enjoys his full constitutional rights. If a Negro baby is born - and this is true also of Puerto Ricans and Mexicans in some of our cities - he has about one half as much chance to get through high school as a white baby, he has one third as much chance to get through college as the white student, he has about a third as much chance to be a professional man, about half as much chance to own a house, he has about four times as much chance that he'll be out of work in his life as the white baby.

I think we can do better. I don't want the talents of any American to go to waste.

I know that there are those who say that we want to turn everything over to the government.

I don't at all.
I want the individuals to meet their responsibilities.
And I want the states to meet their responsibilities,
but I think there is also a national responsibility.

The argument has been used against every piece of social legislation in the last twenty-five years.
The people of the United States, individually, could not

have developed the Tennessee Valley, collectively they could have.

A cotton farmer in Georgia or a peanut farmer or a dairy farmer in Wisconsin or Minnesota, he cannot protect himself against the forces of supply and demand in the market place, but working together in effective governmental programs he can do so.

Seventeen million Americans who live over sixty-five on an average social security check of about seventy-eight dollars a month, they're not able to sustain themselves individually, but they can sustain themselves through the social security system.

> I don't believe in big government, but I believe in effective governmental action.

And I think that's the only way that the United States is going to maintain its freedom, it's the only way that we're going to move ahead.

I think we can do a better job. I think we're going to have to do a better job, if we are going to meet the responsibilities which time and events have placed upon us. We cannot turn the job over to anyone else. If the United States fails, then the whole cause of freedom fails. And I think it depends in great measure on what we do here in this country.

The reason Franklin Roosevelt was a good neighbor in Latin America was because he was a good neighbor in the United States, because they felt that the American society was moving again. I want us to recapture that image. I want people in Latin America and Africa and Asia to start to look to America to see how we're doing things, to wonder what the President of the United States is doing, and not to look at Khrushchev or look at the Chinese communists. That is the obligation upon our generation. In 1933 Franklin Roosevelt said in his inaugural that this generation of Americans has a rendezvous with destiny. I think our generation of Americans has the same rendezvous.

The question now is:

Can freedom be maintained under the most severe attack
it has ever known.
I think it can be. And I think in the final analysis
it depends upon what we do here.
I think it's time America started moving again.

NIXON'S OPENING STATEMENT

(Orthographic Transcription)

The things that Senator Kennedy has said many of us can agree with.

There is no question but that we cannot discuss our internal affairs in the United States without recognizing that they have a tremendous bearing on our international position.
There is no question but that this nation cannot stand still, because we are in a deadly competition - a competition not only with the men in the Kremlin but the men in Peking.

We're ahead in this competition, as Senator Kennedy I think has implied, but when you're in a race the only way to stay ahead is to move ahead.

And I subscribe completely to the spirit that Senator Kennedy has expressed tonight - the spirit that the United States should move ahead.

Where then do we disagree?

I think we disagree on the implication of his remarks tonight and on the statements that he has made on many occasions during his campaign to the effect that the United States has been standing still.
We heard tonight, for example, the statement made that our growth in national product last year was the lowest of any industrial nation in the world. Now last year, of course, was 1958. That happened to be a recession year, but when we look at the growth of GNP this year - a year of recovery - we find that it is six and nine tenths per cent and one of the highest in the world today. More about that later.

Looking then to this problem of how the United States should move ahead and where the United States is moving, I think it is well that we take the advice of a very famous campaigner: Let's look at the record.

> Is the United States standing still?
> Is it true that this Administration, as Senator Kennedy has charged, has been an Administration of retreat, of defeat, of stagnation?
> Is it true that as far as this country is concerned - in the field of electric power, in all of the fields that he has mentioned - we have not been moving ahead?

Well, we have a comparison that we can make. We have the record of the Truman Administration of seven and a half years, and the seven and a half years of the Eisenhower Administration. When we compare these two records in the areas that Senator Kennedy has discussed tonight, I think we find that America has been moving ahead.

Let's take schools. We have built more schools in these last seven and a half years than we built in the previous seven and a half, for that matter in the previous twenty years.
Let's take hydroelectric power. We have developed more hydroelectric power in these seven and a half years than was developed in any previous Administration in history.
Let us take hospitals. We find that more have been built in this Administration than in the previous Administration. The same is true of highways.

Let's put it in terms that all of us can understand. We often hear Gross National Product discussed and, in that respect, may I say that when we compare the growth in this Administration with that of the previous Administration, that then there was a total growth of eleven per cent over seven years, in this Administration there has been a total growth of nineteen per cent over seven years. That shows that

there's been more growth in this Administration than in its predecessor.
But let's not put it there, let's put it in terms of the average family:

What has happened to you? We find that your wages have gone up five times as much in the Eisenhower Administration as they did in the Truman Administration.
What about the prices you pay? We find that the prices you pay went up five times as much in the Truman Administration as they did in the Eisenhower Administration.
What's the net result of this? This means that the average family income went up fifteen per cent in the Eisenhower years as against two per cent in the Truman years.

Now, this is not standing still.

But good as this record is, may I emphasize it isn't enough. A record is never something to stand on, it's something to build on. And in building on this record, I believe that we have the secret for progress - we know the way to progress. And I think first of all our own record proves that we know the way.

Senator Kennedy has suggested that he believes he knows the way. I respect the sincerity with which he makes that suggestion. But, on the other hand, when we look at the various programs that he offers, they do not seem to be new, they seem to be simply retreads of the programs of the Truman Administration which preceded it. And I would suggest that during the course of the evening he might indicate those areas in which his programs are new, where they will mean more progress than we had then.

What kind of programs are we for?
We are for programs that will expand educational opportunities, that will give to all Americans their equal chance for education, for all of the

things which are necessary and dear to the hearts of our people. We are for programs, in addition, which will see that our medical care for the aged is much better handled than it is at the present time.

Here again, may I indicate that Senator Kennedy and I are not in disagreement as to the aim. We both want to help the old people, we want to see that they do have adequate medical care. The question is the means. I think that the means that I advocate will reach that goal better than the means that he advocates.

I could give better examples, but for whatever it is - whether it's in the field of housing or health or medical care or schools or the development of electric power - we have programs which we believe will move America, move her forward and build on the wonderful record that we have made over these past seven and a half years.

Now, when we look at these programs, might I suggest that in evaluating them we often have a tendency to say that the test of a program is how much you're spending. I will concede that in all the areas to which I have referred Senator Kennedy would have the Federal Government spend more than I would have it spend. I costed out the cost of the Democratic platform. It runs a minimum of thirteen and two tenths billion dollars a year more than we are presently spending to a maximum of eighteen billion dollars a year more than we're presently spending. Now the Republican platform will cost more too. It will cost a minimum of four billion dollars a year more, a maximum of four and nine tenths billion dollars a year more than we're presently spending.

Now, does this mean that his program is better than ours?

Not at all. Because it isn't a question of how much the Federal Government spends, it isn't a question of which government does the most, it's a question of which Administration does the right things. And in our case I do believe that our programs will stimulate the creative energies of a hundred and eighty million free Americans. I believe the programs that Senator Kennedy advocates will have a tendency to stifle those creative energies. I believe, in other words, that his programs would lead to the stagnation of the motive power that we need in this country to get progress.

The final point that I would like to make is this:

Senator Kennedy has suggested in his speeches that we lack compassion for the poor, for the old and for others that are unfortunate. Let us understand throughout this campaign, that his motives and mine are sincere. I know what it means to be poor, I know what it means to see people who are unemployed. I know Senator Kennedy feels as deeply about these problems as I do. But our disagreement is not about the goals for America, but only about the means to reach those goals.

EMPIRICAL DATA

Our empirical data is taken from Kennedy's and Nixon's opening statements in the 1960 presidential debates. It is arranged alphabetically according to discourse devices.[130] The examples we list will overlap to some extent. This is due to the fact that an example functioning as say an antithesis can simultaneously function as a restatement. Where these overlapping functions are obvious, we will (for reasons of economy and transparency) try to avoid listing the respective example twice. We use the following notation to indicate whether the example is taken from Kennedy's or Nixon's opening statement:

K, 1	=	Kennedy's opening statement, line 1.
K, 1-5	=	Kennedy's opening statement, lines 1-5.
N, 1	=	Nixon's opening statement, line 1.
N, 1-5	=	Nixon's opening statement, lines 1-5.

To facilitate the interpretation of our empirical data we refer the reader to the pertinent sections in our analyses.

[130] We use this general term, as not all of the headings to the respective examples are, strictly speaking, discourse patterns, such as FOREGROUNDING, BACKGROUNDING, SPECIFICATION, etc.

ANTITHESIS

ANTITHESIS[131]

A. EXPLICIT ANTITHESIS: Thesis | Antithesis | Page

1)  vs.  104-107

or vice versa[132]

2)  vs.  108-113

or vice versa

[131] We distinguish between two types of antithesis: EXPLICIT and IMPLICIT ANTITHESIS. In an EXPLICIT ANTITHESIS the two parts of the antithesis, i. e. (a) the thesis and (b) the antithesis (cf. ch. 1.2.3.), are explicitly stated. In an IMPLICIT ANTITHESIS only the thesis is explicitly stated, the antithesis must be inferred from the overall context. To help the reader we explicitly state the antithetical counterparts of the implicit antitheses in our empirical data.

[132] The following variants also occur  vs.  and 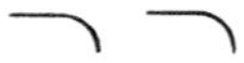 vs.  .

Cf. exs. 6a and b and 8a and b below. The concave rise on *strong* (ex. 3a), *protect himself* (ex. 5a) and *individually* (ex. 6a) signals a grand conclusion. Cf. ch. 2., exs. 27, 35a and 36a in this connection.

B. IMPLICIT ANTITHESIS: Thesis

Thesis	Page
1) [¯¯\ :]	114-115
2) Nuclear stress on modals/grammatical words	116-117
3) 1 ¯¯\ on personal pronouns in the precontour or the postcontour	118-119

Note: Contour type [2] cues a restated antithesis.
Contour type [3] cues a restated antithesis or, more precisely, restated lexical items.

EXPLICIT ANTITHESIS: vs. or vice versa

1a	[2]	[...*the question was* | *whether this* (a) *nation, could ex*-[*ist*]]	K,2-5
1b		[...*the question* (1) *is* | *whether the* [*world will exist*]] (cf. ch. 2., exs. 2a and 2b)	
2a		[*half slave*...	K,3
2b		...*or half* [*free*]] (cf. ch. 2., ex. 2a)	
3a	[3]	[*These are all the things* | ... *that can make, our society* [*strong*]...]	K,83-84
3b		...] *or can mean that it* (a) *stands still*] (cf. ch. 2., ex. 27)	
4a		[..., *individ*(a)*ually* | (a) *could* [*not have developed the Tennessee Valley*]]	K,105-107
4b		[(1) *collectively they* [*could have*]] (cf. ch. 2., exs. 34a and 34b)	

5a [2] [*he cannot pro-* [*tect himself*]...] K,109-112
1

5b [2] [*but working together* | ...[...] *he can do so*] (cf. ch. 2., exs. 35a and 35b)
1

6a [3] [*they're not able* | *to sustain themselves* | *indi-* [*vidually*]] K,115-117
a

6b [3] [*but they can sustain themselves* | *through the social security*
a

[*system*]] (cf. ch. 2., exs. 36a and 36b)

7a [3] [..., *last* [*year*] *was the lowest of any industrial nation* N,23-29

in the world]
f

7b [*but when we look* | *at the growth of GNP,* [*this year*]...] [*we find*
1

that it is ... one of the [*highest*] *in the world today*]
1

(cf. ch. 3., exs. 15a, 15b, 17a and 17b)

8a [3] [... of how the United States, [should | move ahead]] N,30-32
1

8b [3] [and where the United States [is moving]] (cf. ch. 3., exs. 20 and 21)
1

9a [3] [that [then] there was a total growth | of eleven per cent | N,65-68
1

over seven years]

9b [in this Administration | there has been a total growth of

nine- [teen per cent] over seven years]
1

10a [...the average family income | went up [fifteen per cent, in N,81-84

the Eisenhower years]...]

10b ...] as against two per cent, in the Truman years]

11a [2] [But, good as this record [is] N,86-87
1 a

11b *may I emphasize, it isn't enough*] (cf. ch. 3., ex. 37)
a a

EXPLICIT ANTITHESIS: vs. or vice versa

1a [2] [*whether it will move in the direction* | *of* [*freedom*]] K,7-9
:

1b [2] [*or whether it will move in the direction of* [*slavery*]] (cf. n. 68)
a
f

2a [3] [*This is a great* [*country*]] K,45-46

2b [3] [*but I think it could be a* [*greater*] *country*] (cf. ch. 2., exs. 25a and 25b)
a

3a [2] [*And this is a* [*powerful country*]] K,47-48
:

3b [3] [*but I think it could be* | *a more* [*powerful* | *country*]] (cf. ch. 2., exs. 26a and 26b)
a- a

4a [3] [*I don't* | *believe in* [*big government*]][133] K,118-119
a :

4b [2] [*but I believe in effective governmental* [*action*]] (cf. ch. 2., exs. 37a and 37b)
a

[133]Note that contour type [3] cues a closure by return in this instance. Cf. our analysis in ch. 2., ex. 37a.

5a [2] [*that this generation of Americans* | *has a rendezvous with* [*destiny*]] K,140-142

1

5b [*I think our generation of Americans* | *has the* [*same rendezvous*]][134]

a a f

6a ...] *the only way* | *to stay ahead,* N,12-13

6b *is to move ahead*] (cf. ch. 3., ex. 9)

a

7a]... *a recession year*] N,25-27

a

7b ...] *a year of recovery*] (cf. ch. 3., exs. 16a and 16b)

8a [... *the record of the* [*Truman Administration*] *of* N,43-46

:

seven and a half years]

8b [2] [*and the seven and a half years* | *of the*

[134]Contour type [2] indicates that Kennedy is restating what Franklin D. Roosevelt once said.

[*Eisenhower Administration*]][135]
f

9a]... *in these last* | *seven and a half years*] [*than we built* N,50-52
a a

9b *in the previous seven and a half* | ... [...]] (cf. ch. 3., ex. 31)

10a [2] [... *more have been built, in this Administration* | N,58-60
:

10b *than in the* [*previous Administration*]] (cf. ch. 3., ex. 33)

11a [2] [... *there's been more growth* [*in this Administration*] N,69-70
a

11b *than in its predecessor*]

12a [2] [*A record is* [*never something to stand on*] N,87-88
1

12b *it's something to build on*][136] (cf. ch. 3., ex. 38)

---

[135] Contour type [2] in this instance and in ex. 10 below functions as a cue for an absence of focus. Cf. n. 117 in this connection.

[136] Note the use of the *reverse echo* to cue the antithetical specification *a record is something to build on.*

13a [...*our* [*own record proves*] *that we know the way*] N,91-93

13b [*Senator Kennedy* | ... [...] ... *believes he knows the way*]

14a [2] ... *Senator Kennedy and I* [*are not in disagreement, as to the* [*aim*]] N,111-115
1 :

14b [2] [*The question is the* [*means*]] (cf. p. 80)
a

15a [2] [*I think that the means* | *that* [*I advocate*] *will reach that goal* | N,115-117
: f

15b *better than the means that he advocates*] (cf. ch. 3., ex. 46)
a f

16a [*Senator Kennedy, would have the spe# Federal Government* [*spend more*] N,129-131
1 a

16b *than I would have it spend*][137]
a

[137]Note the use of the *reverse echo* to cue the specific information that Kennedy, if elected, will be spending more money than Nixon.

17a [3] [*Because it isn't a question* | *of how* [*much*] ...][138] N,142-145

a

[2] [*it isn't a question of ... does the* [*most*]] (= restated thesis)

17b [*it's a question of ... does the* [*right things*]] (cf. p. 83)

a :

18a *our programs* [*will stimulate the cre-* [*ative, energies*]...] N,146-150

1 a :

the programs that Senator Kennedy advocates

18b *will have a tendency, to* [*stifle*] *those creative energies*]

1

(cf. ch. 3., ex. 51 f.)

19a [2] [*I know Senator Kennedy feels* | *as* [*deeply about these problems*] N,160-162

a

19b *as I do*] (cf. p. 85)

---

[138]Note the concave rise on *much* to cue the antithesis, instead of the topical convex fall. It functions as a cue for grand conclusion. Cf. ch. 2., exs. 2b and 10 and n. 69 in this connection.

20a [3] [*But our disagreement, is not about the* [*goals* | *for America*]][139] N,162-164

a a

20b [3] [*but only, about the* [*means* | *to reach those goals*]][140]

1 a f

(cf. ch. 3., ex. 53 and 54)

[139] Note that contour type [3] cues a closure by return in this instance.

[140] Note that contour type [3] cues a closure by return in this instance.

IMPLICIT ANTITHESIS: [:]

1	we ≠ they[141]		*[in the direction of the road that [we are* a : *taking]]* (cf. ch. 2., ex. 4)	K,8
2	these Americans ≠ the other Americans		*[because I don't think* | *we're meeting our obligations, towards [these Americans]]* :	K,64-65
3	moving ≠ standing still	[3]	*[I think it's time* | *America started [moving* a : *again]]*[142] (cf. ch. 2., ex. 43)	K,148
4	spirit ≠ nothing else	[3]	*[And I subscribe* : | *completely, to the* 1 a	N,14

[141] *We* refers to the United States. It is to be understood as antithetical to the Soviet and Chinese communists. Cf. ch. 2., exs. 4 and 5.

[142] Note that contour type [3] cues a closure by return in this instance.

			[*spirit*] ...][143] (cf. ch. 3., ex. 10) :	
5	we ≠ they[144]	[4]	[... *I believe* | *that*, [*we have the* : *secret*] ...] (cf. ch. 3., ex. 39)	N,89
6	expand ≠ cut back on		[*We are for programs* | *that will ex-* [*pand* 1 : : *educational opportunities*]] (cf. ch. 3., ex. 44)	N,103-104
7	all Americans ≠ not just some	[2]	[*that will give to* [*all Americans*] ...] : : (cf. p. 79)	N,104
8	stagnation ≠ animation	[3]	[... *his programs, would lead to the* 1 *stag-* [*nation*] ...] (cf. n. 128) a :	N,151-152

[143]Note that contour type [3] cues a closure by return in this instance.

[144]*We* refers to the Republican Party. It is to be understood as antithetical to the Democratic Party. Cf. ch. 3., ex. 39. Contour type [4] indicates that Nixon is presenting his particular assertion as an apodictic statement.

IMPLICIT ANTITHESIS:		Nuclear stress on modals/grammatical words	
1 we do ≠ they do[145]		[*I think* | *it will depend in great measure* | 1 *upon what* [*we do*]...] (cf. ch. 2., ex. 5)	K,10-11
2 we build ≠ they build[146]	[2]	[*on the kind of society that* [*we build*] ...] (cf. ch. 2., ex. 6)	K,12
3 we have ≠ they have[147]	[2]	[*the kind of society* | [*we have*]] (cf. ch. 2., ex. 12)	K,26
4 Cf. ch. 2., ex. 19		[*Are we doing* | *as much as we* [*can do*]]	K,35
5 Cf. ch. 2., ex. 20	[2]	[*Are we as strong* | *as we* [*should be*]]	K,36
6 Cf. ch. 2., ex. 21	[2]	[*Are we as strong* | *as we* [*must be*]]	K,37

[145] Cf. n. 141.

[146] *Ibid.*

[147] *Ibid.*

			we disagree on ... statements ...	
7	has not been standing still ≠ has been standing still	[2]	[*to the effect that the United States,* : [*has been standing still*]][148] (cf. ch. 3., ex. 12)	N,20-21
8	is not standing still ≠ is standing still		[*Is the United States standing still*] (cf. ch. 3., ex. 22) 1	N,35
9	has been moving ahead ≠ has been standing still	[3]	[*I think we find that America* [*has been moving ahead*]][149] (cf. ch. 3., ex. 27) a : a	N,48-49

[148] Note that the complex nucleus in this ex. and in ex. 8 below serves as a cue for refutation.

[149] Contour type [3] cues a closure by return. See n. 116 in this connection.

IMPLICIT ANTITHESIS:			1 ⌒ on personal pronouns in the precontour or the postcontour	
1	I (Kennedy) ≠ he (Nixon)		[*I think* | *it will depend* ... (cf. ch. 2., ex. 3) 1 ⌒ ‿	K,10
2	Chinese communists ≠ Soviet communists		[*The Chinese communists* | *have always had* ... 1 ⌒ ‿ (cf. ch. 2., ex. 9)	K,21
3	we ≠ they[150]		[*We have built* ... (cf. ch. 3., ex. 31) 1 ⌒	N,50
4	Cf. n. 150		[*We have developed*... (cf. ch. 3., ex. 32) 1 ⌒	N,54
5	we ≠ they[151]	[2]	[*We know the* [*way to progress*]] 1 ⌒ ‿ (= restatement of line 89)	N,90

[150] *We* refers to the Eisenhower Administration. *They* refers to the Truman Administration.

[151] *We* refers to Nixon and his party, i. e. the Republicans. *They* refers to Kennedy and his party, i. e. the Democrats. Cf. ch. 3., ex. 39 in this connection.

6	Cf. n. 151	...] *what kind of programs* | *are we for*] 1 f (cf. ch. 3., ex. 42)	N,102
7	Cf. n. 151	[*We are for programs* | ... (cf. ch. 3., ex. 44) 1 :	N,103
8	Cf. n. 151	[... *we have programs* | ... 1	N,121

APODICTIC STATEMENT

APODICTIC STATEMENT[152]

	Page
Contour Type [4]	122

[152] An APODICTIC STATEMENT is a statement which claims to be necessarily true, i. e. a statement which rules out contradiction. Both Kennedy and Nixon present a number of their particular assertions as apodictic statements. Cf. in particular ch. 2., ex. 15 in this connection.

1 [4] [*If* [*we do* | *well*] *here*] (cf. ch. 2., ex. 15) K,29

2 [4] [*I don't want the talents* | *of* [*any American*] *to go to waste*] K,95-96

3 [4] [*And I think* | *that's the* [*only way that the United States*] *is going to maintain its freedom*] K,120-121
a

4 [4] [*I think we're going* | *to* [*have to do*] *a better job*] (cf. ch. 2., ex. 39) K,123-124

5 [4] [*I* [*think we disagree*] *on the implication of his remarks tonight*] N,18-19
a

6 [4] [*And in building on this record* | *I believe* | *that,* [*we have the secret,*] *for progress*] (cf. ch. 3., ex. 39) N,88-89

7 [4] [*And in our case, I* [*do believe*] *that our programs,*] (cf. ch. 3., ex. 51) N,145-146
a a

CLOSURE BY RETURN

CLOSURE BY RETURN			Page
[3]	$[\dots_a [\quad]]$	Nuclear pitch pattern not specified	125-127

1 [3] [*Therefore* | *I think the question before the American* K,33-34
a

people [*is*]] (cf. ch. 2., ex. 18)

2 [3] [*These are all the things* | *I think in this country that can make,* K,83-84

our society [*strong*] *or can mean that it stands still*] (cf. ch. 2., ex. 27)
a

3 [3] [*I think* | *we can do* [*better*]] (cf. ch. 2., ex. 28) K,95
a

4 [3] [*I don't* | *believe in* [*big government*]] K,118-119
a

[2] [*but I believe in effective governmental* [*action*]] (cf. ch. 2., exs. 37a and 37b)
a

5 [3] [*I think* | *we can do a better* [*job*]] (cf. ch. 2., ex. 38) K,123
a

6 [3] [*If the United States* [*fails*] *then the whole cause of* K,127-128
a a

freedom fails][153]

[153] Kennedy closes by returning to his original statement in l. 32, i. e. *If we fail (the USA), then freedom fails.*

7 [3] [*And I think it depends* | *in great measure* | *on what* K,128-129
a a

[*we do* | *here*] *in this country*] (cf. ch. 2., ex. 41)
a

8 [3] [*The question* [*now is*]] (cf. ch. 2., ex. 40) K,143
a

9 [3] [*And I think in the final analysis* | *it depends, upon* K,146-147
a

what [*we do here*]] (cf. ch. 2., ex. 42)
a

10 [3] [*I think it's time* | *America started* [*moving again*]] (cf. ch. 2., ex. 43) K, 148
a :

11 [3] [*And I subscribe* | *completely, to the* [*spirit*] *that Senator* N,14-15
: 1 a :

Kennedy, has expressed tonight] (cf. ch. 3., ex. 10)

12 [3] [*I think we find that America* [*has been moving ahead*]] (cf. ch. 3., ex. 27) N,48-49
a : a

13 [3] [*This is not standing* [*still*]] (cf. ch. 3., ex. 36) N,85
a

14 [3] [*he might indicate those areas ... [in which, his programs* | N,100

are [new]] (cf. ch. 3., ex. 40)
a

15 [3] [*move her forward* | *and build on the [wonderful record*] *that we* N,122-124
a

have made, over these past seven and a half years][154] (cf. ch. 3., ex. 48)
a

16 [3] [*But our disagreement, is not about the [goals* | *for America*]] N,162-163
a a

(cf. ch. 3., ex. 53)

17 [3] [*but only, about the [means* | *to reach those goals*]] (cf. ch. 3., ex. 54) N,163-164
1 a f

[154]Note the echoing postcontour to cue that Nixon is restating the fact that this *wonderful record* is the result of *seven and a half years* of effort.

CONCESSION

CONCESSION : RESERVATION

		Page
CONCESSION:	[] but ...	130-132

Note: Contour type [2] functions as a cue for

1) absence of focus
2) restatement

Contour type [3] functions as a cue for

1) closure by return
2) restated lexical items

The cue value of contour type [2] and contour type [3] will be indicated to the left of each example.

1			[*We discuss tonight, do-* [*mestic issues*]] *but ...* : a (cf. ch. 2., ex. 8)	K,14
2			[*The Chinese communists* | *have always had* | *a* 1 *large popu-* [*lation*]] *but ...* (cf. ch. 2., ex. 9) a	K,21-22
3	restated lexical item	[3]	[*This is a great* [*country*]] *but ...* (cf. ch. 2., ex. 25a)	K,45
4	restatement	[2]	[*And this is a* [*powerful country*]] *but ...* : (cf. ch. 2., ex. 26a)	K,47
5			[*I want the individuals to meet their* a *responsi-* [*bilities*]] (cf. ch. 2., ex. 31)	K,100
6	restated lexical item	[3]	[*And I want the states* | *to meet* 1	K,101

			[*their responsibilities*]] *but* ... (cf. ch. 2., ex. 32)	
7	closure by return	[3]	[*I don't* | *believe in* [*big government*]] *but* ... a :	K,118
			(cf. ch. 2., ex. 37a)	
8	restatement	[2]	[*We're a-* [*head in this competition*] ...] *but* ... a :	N,11-12
			(cf. ch. 3., ex. 8)	
9	closure by return	[3]	[*And I subscribe* | *completely, to the* [*spirit*] ...] : 1 a :	N,14-15
			(cf. ch. 3., ex. 10)	
10	absence of focus	[2]	[*I respect the sin-* [*cerity*] ...] *but* ... a f	N,93
			(cf. p. 77)	
11	restatement	[2]	... *Senator Kennedy and I* [*are not in* 1	N,111-112

disagreement, as to the [aim]] ... (cf. p. 79f.)
:

12 absence of focus [2] [*I could give [better examples] but for for* #] N,118
f

(cf. ch. 3., ex. 47)

13 [*I will* | *con- [cede]* ...] N,128
1 :

14 restatement [2] [*I know Senator Kennedy feels* | *as [deeply* N,160-162
a

about these problems] as I do] but ... (cf. p. 85)

15 closure by return [3] [*But our disagreement, is not about the* N,162-163
a a

[*goals* | *for America]] but* ... (cf. ch. 3., ex. 53)

PROPOSITION : COUNTERPROPOSITION		Page
COUNTERPROPOSITION:		135-136

Note: Contour type [2] functions as a cue for restatement.

Contour type [3] functions as a cue for

1) closure by return

2) restated lexical items

The cue value of contour type [3] will be indicated to the left of each example.

1			[*If* [*we fail*] *then freedom fails*][155]	K,32
2			[*I want the individuals to meet their* a *responsi-* [*bilities*]] (cf. ch. 2., ex. 31)	K,100
3	restated lexical item	[3]	[*And I want the states* | *to meet* 1 [*their responsibilities*]] (cf. ch. 2., ex. 32)	K,101
4	closure by return	[3]	[*I don't* | *believe in* [*big government*]] a : (cf. ch. 2., ex. 37a)	K,118
5	closure by return	[3]	[*I think it's time* | *America started* a [*moving again*]] : (cf. ch. 2., ex. 43)	K,148

[155] Note Kennedy's shift of the concave fall to the postcontour to background his comment, parallel to exs. 14 and 15. Cf. ch. 2. This example can be interpreted as a counterproposition to *If we do well here, then I think freedom will be secure around the world.*

6 [2] [*A record is* [*never something to stand on*] ...][156] N,87

1

7 ...] *what kind of programs* | *are we for*][157] N,102

1 f

8 [2] ... *Senator Kennedy and I* [*are not in* N,111-112

1

disagreement, as to the [*aim*]][158]

:

9 [*It's a question of which Administration* | N,144-145

a

does the [*right things*]] (cf. p. 83)

:

[156] This example can be interpreted as a counterproposition to the implicit proposition *a record is something to stand on*.

[157] This example can be interpreted as a counterproposition to *what kind of programs Kennedy is for*. Cf. ch. 3., ex. 42 in this connection. The pitch configuration in the postcontour can be interpreted as a positional variant of the configuration topical for counterpropositions.

[158] This example can be interpreted as a counterproposition to *we're not in agreement on the means*.

DENIAL

DENIAL : REFUTATION	Page
DENIAL: The complex nucleus [] on the denial cues the refutation.	139

Note: Contour type [2] functions as a cue for restatement.

1 *[I [know that there are those | who say that] we want to turn* K,97-98

:

everything over to the government][159] (cf. ch. 2., ex. 29)

2 [2] *[I don't | at all]* (cf. ch. 2., ex. 30) K,99

3 *I think we disagree on ... statements ...*

[2] *[to the effect that the United States, | [has been standing still]]* N,21

:

(cf. ch. 3., ex. 12)

4 *[Is the United States standing still]* (cf. ch. 3., ex. 22) N,35

1

5 *Is it true that ...*

...] we have not been moving ahead] (cf. ch. 3., ex. 26) N,41-42

f

6 [2] *[Not at all]* (cf. ch. 3., ex. 50) N,142

[159] The echoing postcontour cues the restatement (i. e. *what some people are saying*) and at the same time reinforces the cue for refutation.

ENUMERATION

ENUMERATION : CLIMAX

	Enumeration	Climax	Page
A. ENUMERATIVE SERIES:			
	[___ ___ ...	[1]]	142-144
B. CLIMACTIC SERIES:	Enumeration	Climax	
	[2] +	[1] [... [1]]	145

ENUMERATIVE SERIES: [... [1]]

1 [*The kind of country* | ... K,25-27

[*The kind of society* | ...

[*The kind of strength* | ...[160]

2 [*Are we doing* | ... K,35-37

[*Are we as strong* | ...

[*Are we as strong* | ...[161]

3 [*I'm not satisfied to have* | ... *unused*] K,49-94

[*I'm not satisfied* ... *world*]
a

---

[160] Cf. ch. 2., exs. 11, 12 and 13 in this connection.

[161] Cf. ch. 2., exs. 19, 20 and 21.

[*I'm not satisfied* ... *individual*]
a

[*I'm not satisfied* ... *we are*]
a

[*I'm not satisfied* ... *part time shifts*]
a

[*I'm not satisfied* ... *free*]
a

[*I'm not satisfied* ... fullest]
a

[*These are all the things* | ... *stands still*]
a

[*I'm not satisfied* ... *full constitutional rights*][162]
a

4 [2] [*has been an Administration of retreat, of defeat,* N,37-38
a

of stag- [*nation*]][163]
a

[162] Cf. pp. 47-48 in this connection.

[163] Contour type [2] serves as a cue of restatement in this example. Cf. ch. 3., ex. 25 in this connection.

5 [*for whatever it is* | *whether it's in the field of housing,* N,119-121
: :

or health, or medical care, | *or schools, or the # development*

of electric power, we have programs, | *which we believe, will,*
1 a

[*move America*]] (cf. ch. 3., ex. 47)
1

CLIMACTIC SERIES: [2] + [1] [...[1]]

[2] [*Let's take* [*schools*]] N,50-58

[2] [*Let's take hydroelectric* [*power*]]

[1] [*Let us* | *take* [*hospitals*]] (cf. ch. 3., exs. 28, 29 and 30)
1

FOREGROUNDING : BACKGROUNDING

		Page
FOREGROUNDING:	 on the foregrounded element.	148
BACKGROUNDING:	Postcontour position coupled with fadeaway.	149-150

Note: Backgrounding occurs on

1) restated comments
2) digressional phrases
3) the question in *SUBIECTIO*[164]

The cue value of the backgrounding will be indicated to the left of the respective example.

---

[164] Cf. ch. 3., ex. 3 and n. 102 for our discussion of this rhetorical device.

BACKGROUNDING	FOREGROUNDING	BACKGROUNDING	
1	[*The things* ...	...] *many of us* | *can agree with*] f	N,1-2
	that Senator Kennedy has said	(cf. ch. 3., exs. 1 and 2)	
2 digression	[*We're a-* [*head in* a :	*as Senator Kennedy I think has* a	N,11-12
	this competition]	*implied*] (cf. ch. 1.2.3. and ch. 3., ex. 8) f	
	We heard ... that our growth in national product		
3 restated comment	... *last* [*year*]	*was the lowest of any industrial*	N,23-24
		nation in the world] (cf. ch. 3., ex. 13) f	

BACKGROUNDING

1	restated comment	...] *will be the defense of freedom*] (cf. ch. 2., ex. 14) a f	K,28
2	restated comment	...] *then I think* | *freedom will be secure around* *the world*] (cf. ch. 2., ex. 15) a f	K,30-31
3	restated comment	...] *if we're going to maintain* | *our independence*] a (cf. exs. 1 and 2 above)	K,38
4	subiectio	...] *where then* | *do we disagree*] (cf. ch. 3., ex. 3) a f	N,17
5	digression	...] *more about that later*] (cf. ch. 3., ex. 18) f	N,29
6	restated comment	...] *we have not been moving ahead*] (cf. ch. 3., ex. 26) f	N,41-42
7	subiectio	...] *what has happened* | *to you*] a f	N,73

8	subiectio	...] *what about the prices you pay*] a f	N,77
9	subiectio	...] *what's* | *the net result of this*] a f	N,81
10	subiectio	...] *what kind of programs* | *are we for*] (cf. ch. 3., ex. 42) 1 f	N,102
11	digression	...] ... *the final point that I would like to make* | *is this*] (cf. ch. 3., ex. 52) f	N,154

RESTATEMENT

STATEMENT : RESTATEMENT

Note: The echoing postcontour echos the (precontour +) nuclear pitch configuration in the identical order. It frequently co-occurs with a restatement. Where this is the case in the following examples, we will enter the restatement and echoing postcontour as a unit. The co-occurrence will be indicated in the left-hand margin.

RESTATEMENT: [2]

1	echo	[2]	[*on the kind of society that* [*we build*] *on the kind of strength that we maintain*] (cf. ch. 2., exs. 6 and 7)	K,12-13
2		[2]	[*if we meet our obli-* [*gations*]] (cf. ch. 2., ex. 16)	K,29
3		[2]	[*if we're moving a-* [*head*]] (cf. ch. 2., ex. 17)	K,29-30
4		[2]	[*I should make it very clear* | *that I do* [*not think*] *we're doing enough*] (cf. ch. 2., ex. 22)	K,42-43
5	echo	[2]	[*that I am not satisfied as an A-* [*merican*] *with the progress that we're making*][165] (cf. ch. 2., ex. 24)	K,43-44

[165]This example is a restatement of ex. 4 above; the echoing postcontour specifically restates *we're not doing enough*.

6 echo [2] [*it means* | *we're able to sustain our de*- [*fenses*] K,54-56

it means we're able to meet our commitments abroad][166]
f

7 [2] [*it's the only way* | *that we're going to move a*-[*head*]][167] K,121-122
a

8 echo [2] [*without recognizing* | *that they have a tre*- [*mendous* N,4-6
:

bearing] *on our international position*][168] (cf. pp. 59-60)
: f

9 [2] [*a competition not only with the men in the Kremlin* N,9-10
a :

but the men in Pe- [*king*]] (cf. ch. 3., ex. 7)
a

---

[166] This example as a whole is a restatement of ll. 53-54 in Kennedy's opening statement, i. e. of *because economic growth means strength and vitality.*

[167] This example is a restatement of ll. 120-121 in Kennedy's opening statement, i. e. *And I think that's the only way that the United States is going to maintain its freedom.*

[168] This example as a whole is a restatement of ll. 14-17 in Kennedy's opening statement, i. e. *We discuss tonight domestic issues, but I would not want that to be any implication to be given that this does not involve directly our struggle with Mr. Khrushchev for survival.* Cf. ex. 7 on p. 158 and ex. 2 on p. 160.

10 echo [2] [*Now last year of course* | *was nineteen fifty* [*eight*] N,24-26

: a

that happened to be | *a recession year*] (cf. ch. 3., ex. 14)

a

11 [2] [*in all of the fields* | *that he has* [*mentioned*] ...][169] N,40-41

1 a

(cf. p. 70)

12 [2] [*where they will mean* | [*more progress*] *than we had then*] N,100-101

(cf. ch. 3., ex. 41)

13 [2] [*for all of the things* | *which are* [*necessary and* N,105-106

dear] to ...][170] (cf. p. 79)

[169] The example is a restatement of l. 40 in Nixon's opening statement, i. e. *in the field of electric power*. Cf. ex. 10 on p. 158.

[170] This example is a restatement of lines 104-105 of Nixon's opening statement, i. e. *giving all Americans their equal chance for education.*

14 [2] [[*Here again,*] *may I indicate that Senator Kennedy* N,111-112

: a

and I |][171] (cf. p. 79)

[171] Cf. also ex. 14a on p. 111 and ll. 111-115 of Nixon's opening statement for the point Nixon is restating.

RESTATEMENT:		[3]		
1		[3]	[*In the election of nineteen* [*sixty*] ...] a a (cf. ch. 2., ex. 2b)	K,4
2		[3]	[*half* [*slave*]] (cf. ch. 2., ex. 2b) a	K,6
3		[3]	[*or half* [*free*]] (cf. ch. 2., ex. 2b) a 1	K,6
4		[3]	[*the kind of strength* | *we build* | *in the United* [*States*]][172] (cf. ch. 2., ex. 13) 1	K,27
5	echo	[3]	[*even though there* [*is*] *a hungry world*][173] : :	K,58
6		[3]	[*still* [*free*]] (cf. ex. 2 above) 1	K,74

[172]The first occurrence of the lexical item *United States* is in l. 11 of Kennedy's opening statement.

[173]Kennedy is restating a generally known 'truth' in this instance.

7	echo	[3]	[*but that we cannot discuss* | *our in-* [*ternal affairs*] *in the United States*][174] (cf. p. 59f.)	N,3-4
8		[3]	[*There is no* [*question*]] (cf. ch. 3., ex. 5)	N,7
9		[3]	[*Is it* [*true,*] ...] (cf. ch. 3., ex. 24)	N,39
10		[3]	[*in the field of electric* [*power*]][175] (cf. p. 70)	N,40
11	echo	[3]	[*We have built more* [*schools*] *in these last* | *seven and a half years*][176] (cf. ch. 3., ex. 31)	N,50-51
12	echo	[3]	[*We have developed, more hydroelectric* [*power*] *in*	N,54-55

[174] *Internal affairs* is a restatement of *domestic issues*. Cf. l. 14 of Kennedy's opening statement. Cf. also ex. 8 and n. 168 on p. 154.

[175] The first occurrence of the lexical item *power* is in l. 80 of Kennedy's opening statement. Cf. ll. 75-82 of Kennedy's opening statement in this connection.

[176] The first occurrence of *seven and a half years* is in ll. 44-45 of Nixon's opening statement. The echoing postcontour restates this supplementary information. Cf. also ex. 12 below.

these seven and a half years] (cf. ch. 3., ex. 32)
a

13 echo [3] [*Because it isn't a question* | *of how* [*much*] *the* N,142-143
a

Federal Government spends][177] (cf. p. 82f.)
a

[177] The first occurrence of the lexical chain *how much one spends* is in ll. 127-128 of Nixon's opening statement.

RESTATEMENT: Pitch pattern (usually nuclear) on grammatical words.[178]

1 [2] [*I should make it very clear* | *that I do* [*not think*] K,42-43

we're doing enough] (cf. ch. 2., ex. 22)

2 [*but that we cannot discuss* | *our* ...[179] N,3

3 echo [3] [*but that this nation,* [*cannot*] *stand still*][180] N,7-8

(cf. p. 59)

4 [2] [*the spirit that the United States* [*should move* N,15-16

ahead,] ...] (cf. ch. 3., ex. 11)

---

[178] Contour type [2] and [3] serve as additional cues for restatement.

[179] Cf. ex. 8 on p. 154 and ex. 7 on p. 158.

[180] This example is, in particular, a restatement of l. 148 of Kennedy's opening statement, i. e. *I think it's time America started moving again.* The first occurrence of the lexical item *stand still* is in l. 84 of Kennedy's opening statement.

5 [*Looking then* | *to this problem* | *of* ... N,30

(cf. ch. 3., ex. 19)

RESTATEMENT: Echoing postcontour

1 [2] [*but working together* | *in ef-* [*fective governmental* K,111-112
1
programs] *he can do so*] (cf. ch. 2., ex. 35b)

2 [*but when we look* | *at the growth of GNP,* [*this year*] N,26-27
1
a year of recovery] (cf. ch. 3., exs. 15b and 16b)

SPECIFICATION

SPECIFICATION	Page
The reverse echoing postcontour serves as a cue for more specific information.[181] It echos the (precontour +) nuclear pitch configuration in the reverse order.	165-168

Note: Contour type [2] serves as a cue of restatement.

Contour type [3] cues restated lexical items.

[181] The interpretation of the examples given below, i. e. the more specific information being supplied, follows at the end of this section.

1 *[... upon what [we do] here in the United States]* K,11

(cf. ch. 2., ex. 5)

2 *[if we are going to meet the responsibilities | which* K,124-126
1 a

[time and events] have placed upon us] (cf. ch. 2., ex. 39)
f

3 *[and on the statements | that he has [made] on many* N,19-20
a a

occasions during his campaign] (cf. p. 64)

4 [2] *[A record is [never something to stand on] it's* N,87-88
1

something to build on] (cf. ch. 3., ex. 38)

5 *[And I think first of all | our [own record proves]* N,90-91

that we know the way] (cf. p. 76)

6 [*Senator Kennedy* | *has sug-* [*gested*] *that he believes* N,92-93

a a

he knows the way] (cf. p. 77)

7 [2] [*where they will mean* | [*more progress*] *than we had then* ...] N,100-101

(cf. ch. 3., ex. 41)

8 [2] [*that will give to* [*all Americans*] *their equal chance* | N,104-105

: : :

for education] (cf. p. 79)

:

9 [2] [*for all of the things* | *which are* [*necessary and dear*] N,105-107

to the hearts of our people] (cf. p. 79)

10 [*I will* | *con-* [*cede*] *that in all the areas* | *to which* N,128-129

1 : :

I have referred]

11 [*Senator Kennedy, would have the Federal Government* N,129-131
1 a

[*spend more*] *than I would have it spend*] (cf. p. 82)
a

12 [*will stimulate the cre-*[*ative, energies*] *of a hundred and* N,146-148
1 a : :

eighty | *million, free Americans*] (cf. ch. 3., ex. 51)
a

13 [3] [*I believe in other words* | *that his programs, would lead to* N,150-153
a 1

the stag- [*nation*] *of the motive power that we need in this*
a : a 1

country, to get progress] (cf. p. 84)
a

In the preceding examples the *reverse echo* specifies:

1) *we do.*

2) that the American nation has a collective responsibility, which has been imposed upon it by the course of events.

3) when Kennedy has made the statements Nixon is referring to.

4) what one should do with a record.

5) what the Eisenhower record proves, i. e. that Nixon and his party have the *secret for progress.*

6) what Kennedy has supposedly said, i. e. that he has the *secret for progress.*

7) what Nixon's programs will mean for the USA (i. e. ***more*** *progress*) vs. what Kennedy's programs will mean (i. e. ***less*** *progress*).

8) what effect Nixon's programs will have, i. e. they will *give all Americans their equal chance for education.*

9) *necessary and dear* to what, i. e. to the *hearts* of the people of the USA.

10) what areas Nixon's concession applies to.

11) that Kennedy, if elected, will be spending more money than Nixon will.

12) the number of *creative energies* Nixon hopes to *stimulate* with his programs, i. e. *the creative energies of a hundred and eighty million free Americans.*

13) *stagnation.*

DISSERTATION ABSTRACT

This study investigates whether *discourse structure* is signalled by intonational cues and, if so, what these intonational cues are. The empirical motivation for the study was the first joint Kennedy/Nixon election debate in 1960, in particular the opening statements. Our approach is empirical: We a) make observations, b) formulate working hypotheses, and c) test these working hypotheses against additional data, i. e. we rely on further observations to validate or falsify our working hypotheses. Richard M. Nixon, for example, uses a *rising pitch* in his opening statement to cue a *yes-no* question. It was hypothesized that there is a CO-OCCURRENCE RELATION between *rising pitch* and *yes-no* questions. All *yes-no* questions included in our data were taken into account to validate or falsify this working hypothesis. The term CO-OCCURRENCE RELATION was chosen in preference to CORRELATION because the relations were envisaged as many-many relations rather than one-to-one relations. The intonational means at a speaker's disposal for signalling discourse structure are finite. The course of the investigation showed that the functions of the different intonation patterns overlapped - different occurrences of a given intonation pattern functioned as a cue for more than one discourse pattern.

The introduction outlines the principles essential to the organization of an effective discourse: *Unity, coherence* and *emphasis.* The concept of *cohesion* as defined by Halliday/Hasan (1976) accounts for relations in discourse and is functional in what we call *discourse structure.* We postulate an open set of *discourse patterns* including STATEMENT : RESTATEMENT, GENERAL STATEMENT : EXAMPLES, THESIS : ANTITHESIS, CONCESSION : RESERVATION, PROPOSITION : COUNTERPROPOSITION, FOCUS : DIGRESSION, ENUMERATION : CLIMAX and give a short description of the intonational means at a speaker's disposal for signalling discourse structure. This description is based on the model of English intonation proposed by Pilch (1980). We conclude the introduction by stating our working hypothesis: Discourse structure is signalled by a set of intonational cues, which the speaker may (but need not) employ to help convey his message. It is maintained that the speaker runs the risk of producing a piece of discourse which is rhetorically ineffective, if not incoherent, should he choose not to employ the set of intonational cues at his disposal for signalling discourse structure.

Chapters 2 and 3 consist of detailed rhetorical and intonational analyses of the Kennedy/Nixon opening statements. The analyses facilitate the interpretation of the empirical data presented in the appendix. This data, i. e.

the observed and validated *co-occurrence relations* between given discourse patterns and given intonation patterns, is presented in the form of a chart.

BIBLIOGRAPHY

Bartlett, John, *Familiar Quotations*, ed. Christopher Morley and Louella D. Everett, 12th ed. (London, 1949)

Brazil, David, *Discourse Intonation. Discourse Analysis Monographs 1* (Birmingham, 1975)

Brooks, Cleanth, and Robert Penn Warren, *Modern Rhetoric*, 4th ed. (New York, 1979)

Brown, Gillian, *Listening to Spoken English* (London, 1977)

Brown, Gillian, Karen L. Currie, and Joanne Kenworthy, *Questions of Intonation* (London, 1980)

Chafe, Wallace L., "Discourse Structure and Human Knowledge," in *Language Comprehension and the Acquisition of Knowledge*, ed. John Bissel Carrol and Roy O. Freedle (New York, 1972)

Coulthard, Malcolm, and Martin Montgomery, eds., *Studies in Discourse Analysis* (London, 1981)

Couper-Kuhlen, Elizabeth, "Intonational Macrostructures: Aspects of Prosodic Cohesion," BAAL Conference on Intonation and Discourse (Birmingham, 5. April 1982)

Crystal, David, *Prosodic Systems and Intonation in English* (London, 1969)

Crystal, David, and Derek Davy, *Investigating English Style* (London, 1969)

Dieckmann, Walther, *Sprache in der Politik: Einführung in die Pragmatik und Semantik der politischen Sprache* (Heidelberg, 1975)

Dressler, Wolfgang, *Einführung in die Textlinguistik* (Tübingen, 1972)

Esser, Jürgen, *Intonationszeichen im Englischen* (Tübingen, 1975)

Esser, Jürgen, *Englische Prosodie: Eine Einführung* (Tübingen, 1979)

Geißner, Helmut, *Rede in der Öffentlichkeit: Eine Einführung in die Rhetorik* (Stuttgart, 1969)

Geißner, Helmut, *Rhetorik* (München, 1973)

Halliday, M. A. K., *A Course in Spoken English: Intonation* (Oxford, 1970)

Halliday, M. A. K., and Ruqaiya Hasan, *Cohesion in English* (London, 1976)

Hochmuth, Marie K., ed., *A History and Criticism of American Public Address*, vol. 3 (New York, 1965)

Kane, Thomas S., and Leonard J. Peters, eds., *Writing Prose: Techniques and Purposes*, 5th ed. (New York, 1980)

Kenyon, John S., and Thomas A. Knott, *A Pronouncing Dictionary of American English* (Springfield, Mass., 1953)

Ladd, D. Robert, Jr., *The Structure of Intonational Meaning* (PhD diss. Cornell University 1978, Bloomington, 1980)

Lausberg, Heinrich, *Handbuch der literarischen Rhetorik* (München, 1960)

Lausberg, Heinrich, *Elemente der literarischen Rhetorik*, 4th ed. (München, 1971)

Leech, Geoffrey, and Jan Svartvik, *A Communicative Grammar of English* (London, 1975)

Longacre, Robert E., "The Paragraph as a Grammatical Unit," in *Discourse and Syntax: Syntax and Semantics*, ed. Talmy Givón, vol. 12 (New York, 1979), 115-134

Mukařovský, Jan, "Standard Language and Poetic Language," in *A Prague School Reader on Esthetics, Literary Structure and Style*, ed. and trans. Paul Garvin (Washington, D. C., 1964), 17-30

Mulder, Jan W. F., and Sándor G. J. Hervey, *The Strategy of Linguistics* (Edinburgh, 1980)

Nixon-Kennedy Debate: First Joint Radio-TV "President Candidate Debate." Recorded 26 September 1960. Audiovisual Archives Division of the National Archives. 200 803

Pakosz, Maciej, "Intonation and Attitude," *Lingua*, 56 (1981), 153-178

Pike, Kenneth L., *The Intonation of American English* (Ann Arbor, 1945)

Pilch, Herbert, "The Elementary Intonation Contour of English: A Phonemic Analysis," *Phonetica*, 22 (1970), 82-111

Pilch, Herbert, *Empirical Linguistics* (München, 1976)

Pilch, Herbert, "Intonation in Discourse Analysis," *Phonetica*, 34 (1977), 81-92

Pilch, Herbert, English Intonation as Phonological Structure." *Word*, 31 (1980), 55-67

Pilch, Herbert, "Intonation als kommunikative Funktion," in *Festschrift zum 60. Geburtstag von Franz Link*, ed. Ulrich Halfmann, Kurt Müller, and Klaus Weiss (Berlin, 1984) 195-210

Pilch, Herbert, MS. 1, Manual of English Phonetics, Universität Freiburg, Freiburg

Pilch, Herbert, MS. 2, Manual of English Phonetics, Universität Freiburg, Freiburg

Pilch, Herbert, *Manual of English Phonetics* (München, forthcoming)

Plett, Heinrich F., *Einführung in die rhetorische Textanalyse* (Hamburg, 1973)

Quirk, Randolph, Sidney Greenbaum, Geoffrey Leech, and Jan Svartvik, *A Grammar of Contemporary English* (London, 1972)

Schild, Hans-Jochen, *Sprache und Herrschaft: Studien zur Theorie politischer Rhetorik und ihrer zeitgenössischen Praxis in den USA* (Diss. Frankfurt am Main, 1972)

Schopf, Alfred, *Das Verzeitungssystem des Englischen und seine Textfunktion* (Tübingen, 1984)

"Smith, Alfred Emanuel." *Encyclopaedia Britannica* 1953 ed.

Traugott, Elizabeth C., and Mary L. Pratt, *Linguistics for Students of Literature* (New York, 1980)

Webster's New World Dictionary of the American Language, College Edition (New York, 1962)

Wode, Henning, "Englische Satzintonation," *Phonetica*, 15 (1966), 129–218

Young, Richard E., Alton L. Becker, and Kenneth L. Pike, *Rhetoric: Discovery and Change* (New York, 1970)